Cruising Grounds

Cruising Grounds

By the Editors of
TIME-LIFE BOOKS

The

TIME-LIFE Library of Boating

TIME-LIFE BOOKS, NEW YORK

TIME-LIFE BOOKS

Founder: Henry R. Luce 1898-1967

Editor-in-Chief: Hedley Donovan
Chairman of the Board: Andrew Heiskell
President: James R. Shepley

Vice Chairman: Roy E. Larsen

Managing Editor: Jerry Korn
Assistant Managing Editors: Ezra Bowen,
David Maness, Martin Mann
Planning Director: Oliver E. Allen
Art Director: Sheldon Cotler
Chief of Research: Beatrice T. Dobie
Director of Photography: Melvin L. Scott
Senior Text Editors: Diana Hirsh, William Frankel
Assistant Planning Director: Carlotta Kerwin
Assistant Art Director: Arnold C. Holeywell
Assistant Chief of Research: Myra Mangan

Publisher: Joan D. Manley
Associate Publisher: John D. McSweeney
General Manager: John Steven Maxwell
Assistant Publisher, North America: Carl G. Jaeger
Assistant Publisher, International: David J. Walsh
Business Manager: Peter B. Barnes
Promotion Director: Paul R. Stewart
Mail Order Sales Director: John L. Canova
Public Relations Director: Nicholas Benton

The TIME-LIFE Library of Boating

Editorial Staff for Cruising Grounds:
Editor: George Constable
Assistant Editor: Bryce S. Walker
Text Editors: Anne Horan, Wendy Buehr Murphy,
Philip W. Payne
Picture Editor: Elizabeth D. Meyer
Designer: James Eisenman
Staff Writers: Lee Greene, James B. Murphy,
Kate Slate, John von Hartz
Chief Researcher: Myra Mangan
Researchers: Starr Badger, Reese Hassig,
Monica O. Horne, Ellie McGrath, Joyce Pelto,
Wendy A. Rieder, Carolyn Stallworth
Design Assistants: Anne B. Landry (art
coordinator), Rosi Cassano, Joan Hoffman,
Deanna Lorenz
Editorial Assistant: Molly Toal

Editorial Production
Production Editor: Douglas B. Graham
Assistant Production Editor: Feliciano Madrid
Operations Manager: Gennaro C. Esposito
Quality Director: Robert L. Young
Assistant Quality Director: James J. Cox
Associate: Serafino J. Cambareri
Copy Staff: David L. Harrison (chief),
Kathleen Beakley, Charles Blackwell,
Edward B. Clarke, Florence Keith, Pearl Sverdlin
Picture Department: Dolores A. Littles,
Carolyn Turman Chubet
Traffic: Carmen McLellan

The Cover: Borne along by the Caribbean trades, a sloop glides into an anchorage off the Sir Francis Drake Channel in the British Virgin Islands. To starboard stands the hulking shoulder of Tortola, while in the foreground looms one of the waterworn granite boulders that line the southwest coast of Virgin Gorda.

Frontispiece *(pages 6-7):* A cluster of sleek yachts rafts up at sunset in one of the many sheltered coves of Washington's San Juan Islands beneath the snowy eminence of Mount Baker.

The Consultants: Jim Emmett is senior regional editor of *Waterway Guide*. A veteran cruiser of the Atlantic coast and the Great Lakes, he now lives with his wife aboard their trawler-type boat, *Chinook*.

Art Hemenway, a correspondent for *Yachting* magazine, has cruised along the Northwest shores for 40 years. He lives on a houseboat and periodically ventures out to sea on his 42-foot sailboat.

Art Hutchison is editor of the *Port Pilot and Log Book* of the Great Lakes Cruising Club in Chicago, Illinois. A regular hand in big-boat races on the Lakes, he also competes in small-boat events with his own 19-foot Arrow-class sloop.

Red Marston, a freelance sportswriter and author of numerous articles for boating magazines, has cruised the Florida and Gulf waterways for 20 years. He berths his 38-foot powerboat, *Final Edition*, in St. Petersburg, Florida.

Bill Robinson, who has cruised all over the world since his youth, is editor of *Yachting* magazine and the author of more than a dozen books on sailing.

Bob Walters, author of *Cruising the California Delta* and numerous magazine articles on boating, is editorial director of *SEA & Pacific Motor Boat*.

Jack West, staff commodore of the Southern California Cruiser Association, is the author of many books and magazine articles on boating.

Valuable assistance was given by the following departments and individuals of Time Inc.: Editorial Production, Norman Airey; Library, Benjamin Lightman, Lester Annenberg; Picture Collection, Doris O'Neil; Photographic Laboratory, George Karas; TIME-LIFE News Service, Murray J. Gart; Correspondents Gayle Rosenberg (Los Angeles), Marshall Smith (Miami), David Snyder (New Orleans).

Contents

Shorelines for Wanderers

Shorelines for Wanderers

American boatmen are fervent loyalists, devoted not only to their boats but also to the places they sail them. There is hardly a one who will not defend his own particular stretch of coastline, riverbank or lake front as the best cruising ground on earth. A sailor brought up on the coast of Maine will declare an abiding passion for his spruce-topped granite islands—and never mind the billows of chill, dank fog. A Florida man will speak of unceasing sunshine and swaths of open beach washed by waters that never dip anywhere near the 59° reported last January. And a resident of Denver or Albuquerque will tell you that for sheer, overpowering splendor no waters in the world can beat the ones that flow through the middle of the desert, along the impounded lakes and canyons of the Colorado River.

Yet for all their selective vision, U.S. yachtsmen, like a hundred generations of seafarers before them, are a restless, inquisitive lot, in whose bones is bred the compulsion to explore. Accordingly, each year thousands of them weigh anchor and set out for waters they have never seen before. And these latter-day American explorers are uniquely fortunate among the world's boatmen. From the deep fjords and white-hooded peaks of the north Pacific coast to the desert coves of Baja California, from the grassy flats of New Jersey and the Carolinas to the clear cobalt seas of the Caribbean, no other continent affords more different aspects for the boatman to explore. The waters of the Great Lakes alone cover 94,760 square miles. And America's Atlantic shoreline, with all its scalloped bays and inlets, measures more miles than the earth's circumference at the equator.

If he lived as long as Noah, no one could cover every mile of these shorelines. Yet every sailor can explore those miles in his mind and select out for a real cruise—either next year or someday—those places that answer most perfectly his yearnings. In this volume the cruisable waters of North America are divided into eight favorite cruising grounds: the seven discrete geographic regions shown on the larger map at right, and the river systems depicted in the smaller one. Each of these eight cruising venues is itself so extensive and rich in alternatives that to thoroughly sample the cruising possibilities of any one of them would take an average lifetime. And to describe them completely would be at least as great an undertaking. Instead, these pages offer highlighted rundowns on each area, with special attention given to outstanding or representative locales. In sum, they offer any mariner pondering a cruise something of the flavor of each area, a sampling of its charms—and possibly of its perils—and an appreciation of the kind of cruising it offers.

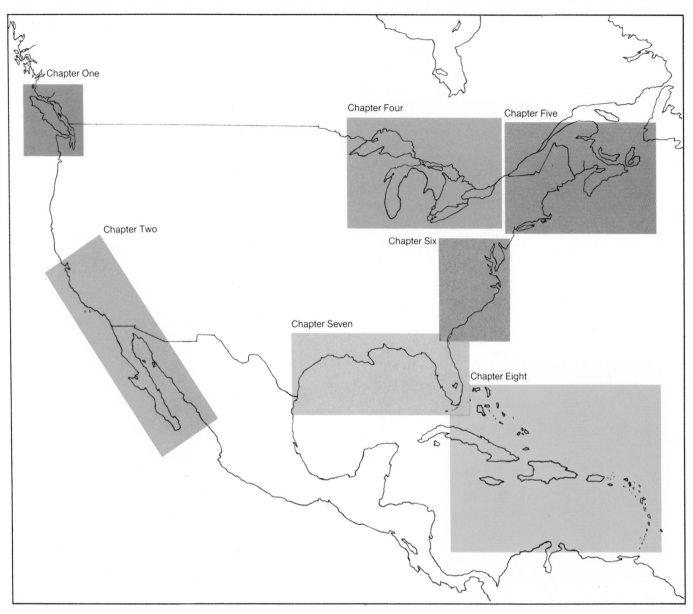

Chapter One

Chapter Four

Chapter Five

Chapter Two

Chapter Six

Chapter Seven

Chapter Eight

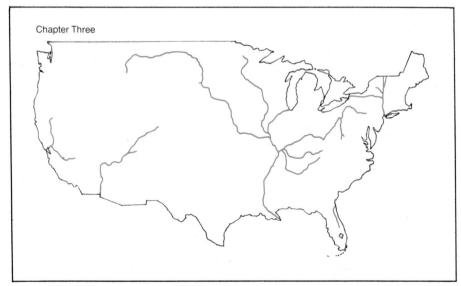

Chapter Three

The major cruising grounds of North America are differentiated by color in these maps and are labeled to indicate the chapter in which they are discussed. They are, on the map above: The Pacific Northwest (dark blue), California and Mexico's Baja (red), The Great Lakes Seaway (green), The Northeast Coast (purple), The Mid-Atlantic Waterways (gray), Florida and the Gulf (light blue), and The Caribbean Islands (yellow). At left, marked in blue, are the Cruising Rivers of America.

1 Late afternoon sun shafts slanted through trees and glanced off rocky islets surrounding Prideaux Haven in British Columbia's Desolation Sound. Fresh-caught salmon sputtered on a barbecue grill aboard our 72-foot powerboat, *Monsoon II.* Off our starboard bow, steaks sizzled on the afterdeck of a Seattle-based cruiser. Ashore, a Vancouver family hunkered down around a small wood fire, hungrily watching a heap of freshly dug clams and oysters as they hissed steam on the way to bursting their shells. No cars, no telephones, no docks, not even a house was visible from where we lay. We basked in the special satisfaction of knowing that when the harbor's transient visitors pushed on the next day, Pri-

THE PACIFIC NORTHWEST

deaux Haven would, for a few hours at least, revert to total wilderness. Just 100 miles by sea from the yacht clubs and marinas of Vancouver, 230 miles from the still more populous yachting center of Seattle, Prideaux Haven is one of the hundreds of unspoiled areas in the Northwest from which a cruising boatman can choose.

I was introduced to Pacific Northwest waters by my husband, Jack, on our honeymoon in 1930. Jack owned an old 38-foot converted pilot boat, and with some innocence we set out under power from Seattle, to Sidney in October, a month that flirts openly with the winter storm season. It was an exciting, sometimes nerve-racking trip for both of us—not the sort of thing generally recommended for honeymoons. Rain and fog dogged us much of the way, and we saw few other pleasure boats. But whenever the sky cleared, the region appeared to us at its most spectacular—the mountains rising overhead, the crisp temperatures of fall adding bright strokes of deciduous color to the thick stands of Douglas fir and Sitka spruce that march along the shore. The beauty of the place seeped into our bones, and even though several years later we moved to Southern California, 1,000 miles away, we have returned to it many times. The journey usually means slugging north into oncoming quartering seas for days on end, until we reach the jutting headland of Cape Flattery. The cape marks the western gatepost to the Strait of Juan de Fuca and the entrance to the northwest cruising grounds, and once we reach it we know the trip has been worthwhile.

On our early explorations, we usually settled for languorous tours through the sheltered waters of Puget Sound. Later we swung north to British Columbia, gradually extending our cruising range on up toward Alaska and adding hundreds of coves, river mouths, fjords and fishing villages to our repertory of familiar and welcoming places.

Deep inside Puget Sound, we've seen people cruising in just about anything that floats—from outboards and houseboats to deep-draft seagoing yachts. One of our favorite inlets in the sound is Hood Canal on the Olympic Peninsula. First stop for us is Hood Head at the entrance for a go at the oysters. Obliging creatures, they lie about at low tide among the pebbles on the beach, not even bothering to hide. From there we motor on past old lumber camps, many of them now sport-fishing retreats; past Potlatch, a large Skokomish Indian reservation; and on to the Great Bend, where the Dungeness crabs swarm in bountiful supply, and where the snowy, saw-toothed skyline of the Olympic range grins over our shoulders, changing color hour by hour.

North of the sound, the San Juan Islands lure us with nine state parks and scores of undeveloped islets where yachtsmen may camp, explore, rock hunt or do whatever else might strike their fancy. Roche Harbor on 15-mile-long San Juan Island is one of the most popular anchorages in the group, and is generally crowded on summer weekends. Operated in the 1880s as a company town by a prosperous lime-quarrying outfit, it played host to hundreds of mer-

Set off by the distant bulk of Mt. Baker, the forested contours of Orcas Island in the San Juans embrace a cove with a ferry slip that receives visitors to the island's resort hotels.

Carolyn West has logged more than 125,000 miles of Pacific coast cruising, from Alaska to Mexico. With her husband, Jack, she has co-authored a detailed sailor's guide called Cruising the Pacific Coast, Acapulco to Skagway. She has also written numerous articles for yachting magazines.

chant and sailing ships. Here and there are relics of the eccentric owner, John Stafford MacMillin, who once ran Roche Harbor as a private fiefdom. Something of a mystic, he built a family mausoleum in a nearby grove—seven 30-foot-high cement columns circling a cement dining table. According to local lore, the six chairs and one ominously empty space are intended to honor his family and to deliver a posthumous rebuke to an unnamed black sheep.

Angling west and north of the San Juans is the Canadian border, its precise location the result of a brief, harmless skirmish in 1858 called The Pig War. A garrison of British redcoats was stationed on San Juan Island, and one of the garrison's porkers broke loose, uprooted an American potato patch and was shot for trespassing. The pig was the war's only casualty. The two sides declared an immediate cease-fire, while some diplomats in Europe sat down to decide who owned the territory. The diplomats awarded the San Juans to the United States, and gave the British Vancouver and the nearby Gulf Islands.

It would have made no difference what they had decided, for today both sides of the line are open to all. We often power across to put in at Victoria on the southern end of Vancouver Island. Bustling, flower-bedecked and very civilized, Victoria started out as a regional headquarters of the Hudson's Bay Company and later became a supply point for the Fraser River gold rush. It's a great place to stop if you feel like dressing up or dining elegantly.

Most people cruise British Columbia for the wild grandeur of its mountain scenery. For our money the most spectacular spot is Princess Louisa Inlet *(pages 24-25)* on the mainland side of the Strait of Georgia. For 25 years the inlet was presided over by a genial bachelor named James MacDonald, who purchased a goodly part of the shoreline and lived there summers in a small camp. Mac personally entertained just about every yachtsman who made the 45-mile passage upstream from the strait, apparently on the theory that anyone who loved the place enough to come all that way was automatically a friend of his. Some years ago he deeded the property to an association of local yachtsmen, who turned it over to the government with the proviso that it would always remain wild.

Amid the grandiose perspectives of British Columbia, Jack and I find special pleasure in the rural charm of the tiny local fishing villages, particularly in the archipelagoes in and around Johnstone Strait, northwest of the Strait of Georgia. On Minstrel Island, the town's one general store seems to carry just about everything a cruising customer might want, from food and fuel down to the critical nut, screw or bolt to keep the boat running. This is an easy area to get lost in, however, for so many of the islands and islets look alike at a distance; buoys are few and far between, and the fog settles in like a great gray quilt. I remember one trip from Minstrel to Malcolm Island, in Queen Charlotte Strait, when the fog was so heavy that we could barely make out our own bow staff. We crept along for four hours with compass and stop watch until, utterly exhausted from the tension of watching and listening for the surge of water against unseen islets, we called a halt. Jack picked up a long string of kelp and tied a line to it—a fine temporary anchor that allowed us to rest, recoup our energies and then push on to our destination.

For a mariner who has the time to adventure in the northern reaches of British Columbia, the rewards are great: stopovers like Sointula, a cordial Finnish settlement on Malcolm Island with a fine little restaurant and public sauna; Alert Bay, on smaller Cormorant Island, where the Kwakiutl Indians still carve totem poles; and Village Bay on Hope Island, where the pine coffins of departed Kwakiutl braves are laid to rest in the branches of stubby trees. Here is wilderness cruising at its rugged and remote best, the tree line low on the flanks of the mainland mountains, the late evening sun igniting the snowfields on the glaciated peaks. The beauty and the quiet have cast a spell that we will never shake loose, and we will keep going back and back again, for as long as we are able.

by Carolyn West

The spinnaker of a cruising sloop fills to a gentle northwest breeze as the vessel runs south along Seattle's Shilshole Bay. Beyond the shoreline lie the 7,000-foot peaks of the Olympic range, site of the wildest and most extensive coniferous rain forest in the U.S.

Northwest Passages

The Pacific Ocean, reaching 80 miles inland through the stormy Strait of Juan de Fuca, has created two all-but-landlocked seas, one in the United States, the other in Canada. The southern basin is Puget Sound, outlined in blue on the large map *(right)*, as are the other recommended cruising areas discussed in these chapters. Puget Sound fills an ancient geological depression that was carved out by glaciers one million years ago. Extending inland between the Cascade and Olympic mountain ranges, the sound encompasses 2,000 square miles of sheltered waterway, some 300 islands—and more pleasure craft than any area of comparable size in the Western United States.

The Strait of Georgia, to the north, runs 115 miles along the lee of mountain-spined Vancouver Island, probing deeply into the rocky mainland in a series of spectacular fjords. Between the strait and Puget Sound lies the ragged cluster of the San Juan Islands, with their heavily wooded hillsides, abrupt rocky cliffs and sandy beaches.

To a visitor entering from the Pacific, each of these two inland seas seems to reach indefinitely into the North American continent. So powerful is the impression of a limitless waterway that early explorers in the region believed they had stumbled upon the long-sought Northwest Passage across North America. Indeed, the legend that a passage existed sprang up, in part, from the wild tales of a Spanish sea captain, Juan de Fuca, who claimed discovery in 1592 of "a broad Inlet of sea between 48 and 49 degrees of latitude" surrounded by snow-capped peaks. De Fuca described in perfect detail the strait that now bears his name, but no one knows where he got his information; he had never been north of Acapulco.

The legend of the inland sea persisted for two centuries. Then in 1792 England's George Vancouver, who had sailed past the strait in 1779 as a midshipman under Captain Cook, returned to circumnavigate Vancouver Island and draw up the first set of accurate charts. The only outlet, the charts revealed, led northwest through the Johnstone and Queen Charlotte straits, sending the traveler right back to the Pacific, en route to Alaska.

While he was exploding the myth of a Northwest Passage, Vancouver also became an unequivocal booster for the area. "Nothing can be more striking than the beauty of these waters," he wrote in his journal. "There is no country in the world that possesses waters equal to these."

HOPE ISLAND
QUEEN CHARLOTTE STRAIT
MALCOLM ISLAND
CORMORANT ISLAND
JOHNSTONE STRAIT
VANCOUVER

PACIFIC OCEAN

Miles
0　　　　25　　　　50

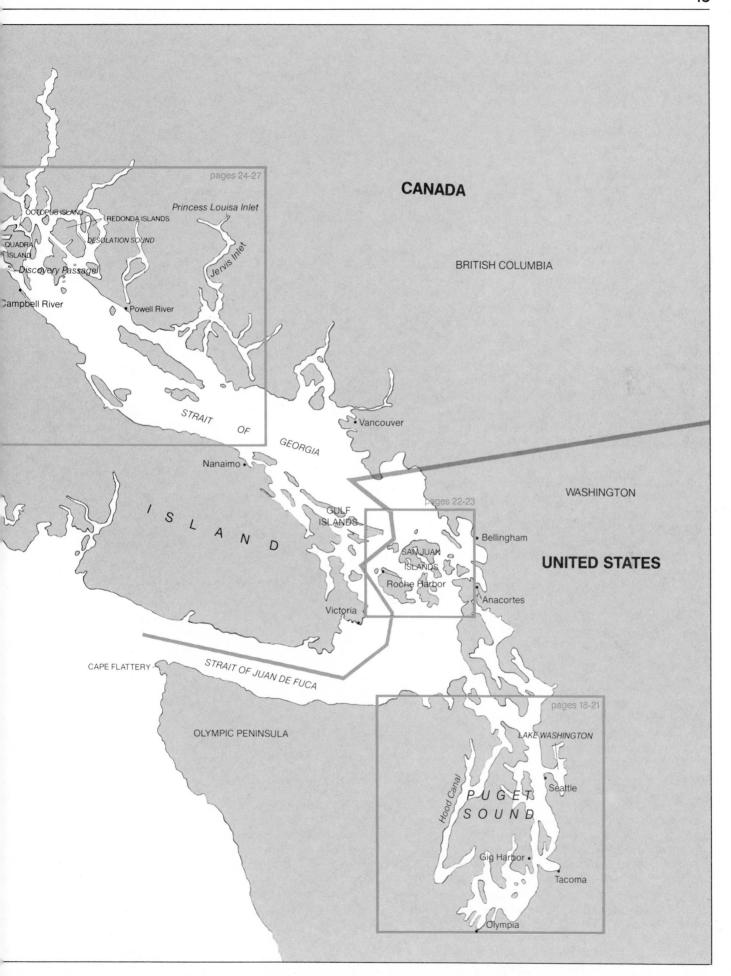

CANADA

BRITISH COLUMBIA

WASHINGTON

UNITED STATES

pages 24-27

Princess Louisa Inlet

OCTOPUS ISLAND

REDONDA ISLANDS

DESOLATION SOUND

QUADRA
ISLAND

Jervis Inlet

Discovery Passage

Campbell River

Powell River

STRAIT   OF   GEORGIA

Vancouver

Nanaimo

ISLAND

GULF
ISLANDS

pages 22-23

SAN JUAN
ISLANDS

Bellingham

Roche Harbor

Anacortes

Victoria

CAPE FLATTERY

STRAIT OF JUAN DE FUCA

OLYMPIC PENINSULA

pages 18-21

LAKE WASHINGTON

Hood Canal

PUGET
SOUND

Seattle

Gig Harbor

Tacoma

Olympia

Winds and Weather

No place in North America carries such a grim reputation for gray skies and rainy days as does the Pacific Northwest. Oddly enough, for the boatman this reputation poses no threat. Most of the rain falls after the end of the May-to-September boating season; and even then, the only severe rainstorms occur on the western slopes of the Olympic Mountains, where moist prevailing westerlies blow in from the Pacific to dump as much as 142 inches a year. But to leeward of the Olympics in Puget Sound, rainfall averages only 48 inches—no more than along the coast of New England. In the Strait of Georgia, it is slightly heavier —about 60 inches a year. But throughout these waters, only the winters are rainy; summers are relatively dry, with only about six wet days a month.

Fog is another matter. Dense day-long fogs may settle in the Strait of Juan de Fuca at any time of year. On Puget Sound and the Strait of Georgia, the fog that builds up on summer evenings usually burns off by morning. But from October onward, the fogs thrive on cool weather and may hold on for days at a time.

Wind direction and speed fluctuate considerably, with the summer's prevailing westerlies often shifting to southeasterlies, causing temperatures to jump from the average of 70° up into the 80s. But summer storms sometimes come whipping in from Alaska with 25-knot winds and chilling rain dropping temperatures more than 20° in minutes. Visiting sailors should pack sweaters and sea boots with their regular gear.

Tides and Currents

Tide levels throughout the region range from nine feet in open water and up to 15 feet at the heads of narrow bays and estuaries. In a few places tidal currents can be severe. They run from two to four knots in Juan de Fuca, up to five knots in Haro and Rosario straits on either side of the San Juan Islands and at the entrance to Puget Sound, building to eight knots in narrow Deception Pass, a main route between Puget Sound and the San Juan Islands. Some of the strongest tidal flows in North America occur in the narrow channels off the Strait of Georgia. These include the nine-knot peak current at the entrance to Princess Louisa Inlet *(pages 24-25)* and the 12-knot surge at Seymour Narrows along the approach to the Octopus Islands *(pages 26-27)*.

Pilotage

Puget Sound and the Strait of Georgia are deep and quiet for the most part, with soundings ranging from 150 to 1,200 feet and no heavy swells. The Strait of Juan de Fuca, however, can be tough going, especially in a northwesterly. Occasional rocks and reefs in the narrow passages between islands—combined with the region's strong currents—can make piloting difficult in restricted areas. But main channels and harbor entrances are generally wide and well marked, in both U.S. and Canadian waters. Note that while Canadian buoyage systems are quite similar to those used in the United States, boats traveling in Canadian waters must observe the international right-of-way rules.

Perhaps the worst navigational hazard here is other boats. The waters churn to a stream of commercial traffic, including freighters, fishing boats and one of the greatest concentrations of tugboats in the world, which haul everything up to and including half-mile-long log booms. Pleasure craft should avoid the main shipping lanes, marked on charts as Vessel Traffic Systems, whenever possible. These lanes are particularly dangerous during heavy rain, when visibility drops to a quarter mile, and in

fog, when it falls below 50 feet. In fact, when planning a cruise, it is wise to include several layover days to avoid traveling in fog or rain. Even in good weather, it is a good idea for powerboatmen to proceed at less than 10 knots, while keeping a sharp lookout to avoid another local danger—collision with the thousands of partially submerged logs that have escaped from tows.

Boats and Special Equipment

Boats of almost every size and variety cruise here. Small trailered outboards and day sailers cruise in Puget Sound and Lake Washington, as well as in the protection of the Strait of Georgia, while stouter craft can take on the often rough waters of the Strait of Juan de Fuca. Sailboats should be equipped with dependable auxiliary engines for any constricted area such as the Hood Canal, the San Juan Islands, and the Octopus and Redonda islands, where lofty headlands may cause local winds to be fluky and unreliable.

Most anchorages are deep and offer good holding ground. Boats should carry stockless anchors, like the Danforth or CQR plow, that are less likely to foul as the vessels drift around their anchor rodes with the changing tides. It is a good idea to carry a second anchor to keep the stern from swinging in crowded anchorages. In some spots boatmen prefer a line of 200 feet or more that can be used to secure the stern to a rock or tree ashore.

Bring along a good VHF radio receiver to pick up marine weather broadcasts from stations in Puget Sound and British Columbia. A dependable RDF will simplify piloting in open water during fog, though reception is poor in constricted areas such as inlets and estuaries. A radar reflector is essential. Excellent marine weather reports along with warnings of navigational hazards and emergency messages to local ships are transmitted on 1630 kHz in Canada and on 2670 kHz in the United States.

Also useful are rakes, small shovels and old shoes for clamming expeditions, and a portable kerosene stove or charcoal grill for shore cooking, since fires are forbidden on many beaches.

Wildlife

The Pacific Northwest, a major flyway for migratory birds, teems with transient bird life: snow geese, mallards, black brants, grebes and peregrines. Indigenous species include rhinoceros birds, murres, leaf sandpipers, grouse and scores of bald eagles, which feed on the Belgian hare of the San Juan Islands.

Herds of harbor seals proliferate throughout the region. They are sometimes pursued by packs of killer whales that circle Vancouver Island, mostly in the winter. And black-tailed deer, cougars and black bears can often be seen foraging along the forested shoreline.

Sports

The region boasts some of the world's best sport fishing, with most anglers preferring to go for two types of salmon: Chinooks, which average 20 to 25 pounds apiece, and cohos, which run from seven to 10 pounds. Chinook season is in August, when the big fish head for spawning grounds in the Campbell River. Cohos can be found in open water, particularly in Puget Sound, from spring through fall. Three other kinds of salmon—sockeye, humpback and chum—bite a hook less readily but still make good eating. Medium-weight rods, reels and line are needed for salmon fishing.

A Washington Department of Fisheries permit is required for salmon fishing in Puget Sound or the San Juan Islands. In Canadian waters, British Columbia demands a permit not only for fishing but also for clamming, crabbing and oyster picking. The permit is available from the License Section of the Canadian Fisheries Service, and its cost is based on boat length.

The relatively warm waters of Puget Sound and the Strait of Georgia provide good swimming, scuba diving and water-skiing—though care should be taken not to swim in areas with strong currents. Swimming in the San Juans is for the warm blooded and courageous: temperatures run about 55°.

Regional Boating Regulations

U.S. boats and equipment that meet Coast Guard standards can be legally operated in Canadian waters after a cruising permit has been obtained from Canadian customs offices at Victoria, Vancouver, Sidney, Nanaimo, New Westminster, Campbell River, Powell River or Bedwell Harbor. Upon returning to U.S. waters, the boat must be cleared by U.S. customs authorities at Friday Harbor or Roche Harbor on San Juan Island, or at Bellingham, Anacortes, Port Townsend, Blaine, Everett, Port Angeles or Seattle.

In Canada it is customary to fly the Canadian ensign from the starboard spreader or from the jack staff. U.S. dollars are acceptable at most stores and marinas. Remember, however, that Canadian fuel is sold by the imperial gallon, which is 20 per cent larger than the U.S. gallon.

Major Provisioning Ports

The following ports, listed from south to north, are the principal departure points and provisioning centers for Pacific Northwest cruising. All offer sheltered marina moorage within easy reach of fuel pumps, marine-supply stores, supermarkets, laundries and, should the need arise, repair yards and hospitals.

Seattle: The Northwest's largest metropolis (population 500,000) and the chief base for cruises into Puget Sound or Lake Washington.
Victoria: The capital of British Columbia, with three harbors—a convenient port of call for boats using Haro Strait, the main route between the straits of Georgia and Juan de Fuca.
Anacortes: A favorite jump-off spot for exploring the nearby San Juan Islands, and the U.S. terminal for the islands' ferry service.
Friday Harbor: On San Juan Island, the principal port in the archipelago, and a convenient port of entry for boats returning from Canada.
Bellingham: The northernmost U.S. provisioning center for cruises into the San Juan Islands and the Strait of Georgia.
Nanaimo: A lumber and fishing port on the western shore of the Strait of Georgia, linked by ferry to the city of Vancouver, and Vancouver Island's main supply depot.
Vancouver: The third largest city in Canada and the commercial center of British Columbia; also a popular provisioning base for cruises into the Strait of Georgia.
Powell River-Westview: Adjoining towns that provide the most extensive marine facilities in the northeastern portion of the Strait of Georgia.
Campbell River: A logging town on Vancouver Island noted as a commercial and sport-fishing cen-

ter; the last spot for extensive provisioning before cruising into the supply-short northern islands beyond the Strait of Georgia.

Coast Guard Stations

The 13th Coast Guard Division, based in Seattle, maintains an air-rescue base at Port Angeles and shore stations near Port Townsend, Bellingham, Anacortes, Everett and Gig Harbor.

The Canadian Coast Guard operates cutters and helicopters from Vancouver and Victoria, and also runs boat patrols during the summer among the Gulf Islands and in the Strait of Georgia.

Charts and Publications

The general area is covered by U.S. National Ocean Survey charts 6401 and 6380 and by Canadian chart 3001, by Volume III of the light lists, by Marine Weather Service Chart MSC-10 and by the West Coast tide tables. Tidal current charts are available for Puget Sound and the Strait of Georgia. Piloting information is contained in these publications: *British Columbia Pilot Vol. I, Southern Portion of the Coast of British Columbia,* and *United States Coast Pilot 7, Pacific Coast.* For the applicable harbor charts, consult National Ocean Survey *Nautical Chart Catalog 2* and *Canadian Nautical Charts, Bulletin 13.* Note that U.S. and Canadian charts use a slightly different system of markings and abbreviations. The most recent revisions of charts can be obtained in principal ports and from the appropriate agencies of the Canadian and United States governments:

Defense Mapping Agency Depot
5801 Tabor Avenue
Philadelphia, Pennsylvania 19120

National Ocean Survey
Distribution Division, C44
6501 Lafayette Avenue
Riverdale, Maryland 20840

Hydrographic Chart Distribution Office
Department of the Environment
1675 Russell Road
Ottawa, Ontario, Canada, K1A0E6

For this area, up-to-date piloting and cruising guides are:

Berssen, Capt. William, USCGR (Ret.), *Pacific Boating Almanac, Pacific Northwest Edition.* Ventura, Calif.: William Berssen Publications.
British Columbia Small Craft Guide, Gulf Islands, Sooke to Nanaimo, Vol. I, Second Ed. Ottawa: Dept. of the Environment.
Calhoun, Bruce:
Cruising the San Juan Islands. Terre Haute, Ind.: SEA Books.
Northwest Passages, Vol. II. Terre Haute, Ind.: SEA Books.
Evergreen Cruising Atlas. Seattle, Wash.: Bernie Straub Publishing Co.
Morris, Frank, and W. R. Heath, *Marine Atlas,* Vol. I. Seattle, Wash.: Bayless Ent.
West, Carolyn and Jack, *Cruising the Pacific Coast, Acapulco to Skagway.* Terre Haute, Ind.: SEA Books.

Leaving the skyline of downtown Seattle astern, a cabin cruiser heads out of the city's main harbor on Elliott Bay. Heavily used by oceangoing vessels, the harbor offers few overnight facilities for small craft but is only a short run from a 1,250-boat marina complex on adjoining Shilshole Bay. Yachtsmen may tie up briefly at a commercial wharf downtown, however, to shop at Seattle's convenient waterfront marketplace.

A cluster of handsome floating houses lies anchored in Seattle's Portage Bay, a body of open water along the canal linking Puget Sound and Lake Washington. Unlike conventional houseboats, these have neither motors nor hulls. Built on concrete slabs buoyed up by Styrofoam floats, they serve as year-round residences whose owners keep small boats moored alongside for commuting or cruising.

Puget Sound

There is a saying around Puget Sound that a boatman could sail its ice-free waters until he was 100 and never have to anchor twice in the same cove. Indeed, the sound and its adjoining inlets wash an incredible 2,000 miles of shoreline, including wilderness coves, dozens of boat docks, seven marine parks and snug anchorages in fishing villages like Gig Harbor *(overleaf)*—all clustered between such bustling cities as Seattle, Tacoma and Olympia.

Throughout the sound the channels are deep and usually shoal-free. To the west, the 4,000- to 8,000-foot-high Olympic Peninsula cuts the force—and much of the prodigious rainfall—of the Pacific northwesterlies, while the Cascades to the east absorb the brunt of winter northeasters. Although tides range 14 feet or more, generating a five-knot current up north at the sound's entrance, the currents dwindle to a manageable knot or two farther south.

Among the most popular cruising spots is Hood Canal, which, despite its name, is a naturally formed and virtually hazard-free inlet that dead-ends some 50 miles inside the Olympic Peninsula. Each summer night its banks twinkle with the bonfires of hundreds of waterborne campers.

However, the main concentration of pleasure craft is around Seattle, in the yacht clubs and marinas to the west of the town, and in 16-mile-long Lake Washington to the east. This fresh-water lake, 200 feet deep, is reached from Puget Sound by the Lake Washington Ship Canal, a man-made waterway with a set of parallel locks, one for pleasure boats and the other for lumber barges and merchant ships. Its wooded shoreline is rimmed with elegant homes, glittering apartment houses and the University of Washington's football stadium—which has an adjoining marine parking lot for the hundreds of fans who boat to home games.

Under the shoulder of Mount Rainier, the crew of a 30-foot sloop furls her mainsail after a day on Lake Washington. One of the world's busiest boating areas, the fresh-water lake boasts three major yacht clubs, six commercial marinas and at least seven launch ramps for trailerborne craft.

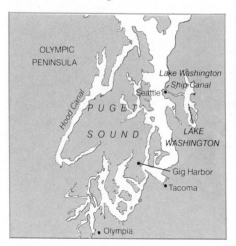

Clammers shovel into the tidal flats of the Hood Canal in search of geoducks (pronounced "gooey-ducks"), big hard-shells that weigh up to seven pounds apiece. Clamming is a popular low-tide pastime throughout the Northwest. The large clams are cut up for fish fries or chowder, while smaller varieties such as Pacific littlenecks and butter clams are generally prepared by being steamed in their shells.

The still waters of Gig Harbor reflect the setting sun's last rays as they strike the snowfields on Mount Rainier, 50 miles southeast. A snug fishing port about 20 miles south of Seattle, Gig Harbor can berth 400 boats in a mile-long inlet whose entrance is less than 100 yards wide. Settled in the 19th Century by Scandinavian, Slavic, Spanish and German homesteaders, Gig Harbor still retains an international flavor among its 1,700 residents—and in such attractions as smörgåsbord restaurants, art galleries, gift shops and a Scandinavian farm museum.

The brown and white floats of a purse-seining net curl over the surface of Puget Sound near Gig Harbor. Widely used by commercial salmon fishermen, who can sometimes take 250 fish with each haul, the net is payed out aft into a circle measuring 500 feet or more in diameter, then drawn tight—called pulling the purse—to haul in the catch. Run out in this manner, the nets will quickly entangle not only fish but also any yachtsman who fails to stay well clear.

The San Juan Islands

Only a day's sail north of Puget Sound lie the 172 San Juan Islands, clustered between the straits of Juan de Fuca and Georgia. The archipelago's rock-bound, richly timbered landscape has scarcely changed since the day George Vancouver first viewed it.

The names of some of the anchorages are reminders of a frequently stormy history. Massacre Bay on Orcas Island was a landing site for the fierce Haida Indians, who rowed over from the mainland in the mid-1800s to attack resident Lummi tribesmen. Smugglers Cove on San Juan Island served as a base for 19th Century diamond smugglers—and in the 1930s as a rendezvous point for bootleggers running whiskey down from Canada.

Today, most of the visitors to the larger islands are resort vacationers who arrive by commercial ferry. But the best cruising is among the smaller and more remote islands, which are accessible only by private boat. A number of these have been set aside by the state of Washington as recreational preserves, among them the ruggedly spectacular Sucia on the archipelago's northern edge. Sucia has six harbors, all with mooring buoys and campsites. The three most popular are Fossil Bay on the south, with the island's only docking facilities; Echo Bay to the east, less developed and open to occasional strong southeast winds; and Shallow Bay on the west, heavily sedimented and best suited for shoal-draft vessels.

The approaches to Sucia are swept by rip tides of up to six knots and studded with unmarked rocks and reefs. It is these reefs, however, that provide one of Sucia's greatest lures—its remarkable tidal pools. When the tide goes out, shallow puddles caught in the rocks teem with trapped shellfish, forming an outdoor aquarium of local marine life—and an unlimited source for a grand seafood feast.

A plateful of blue mussels, gleaned from tidal pools loaded with crabs, scallops, oysters, clams and other mollusks and crustaceans, simmers over an open fire. While mussels can be steamed in sea water, experienced trenchermen prefer to substitute a beaker or two of dry white wine, and to add chopped parsley and shallot or onion. When the shells pop open, the mussels are ready to eat.

A cluster of starfish, temporarily stranded at low water, grips the algae-encrusted slope of a Sucia reef. Voracious salt-water predators, the starfish feed upon shellfish—which in turn are nourished by a rich brew of microscopic plankton that sweeps over them with each new tide. The button-like objects are sea anemones, other plankton eaters that have retracted their tentacles until the tide returns.

Eroded by centuries of tidal grinding, the 150-foot sandstone cliffs of Sucia's Shallow Bay are the most spectacular of the island's land forms. (In the early 1900s, sandstone from Sucia was barged into Puget Sound to pave the streets of Seattle.) Besides its scenic grandeur, Sucia has seven main beaches, five miles of hiking trails and some 50 campsites operated by the park service for yachtsmen who want to tent down ashore for the night.

A great blue heron, one of a protected colony on Sucia, searches the shallow waters of a tidal pool for shellfish trapped by the retreating tide. More than 300 species of birds proliferate in the San Juan Islands, including scoter ducks, golden and bald eagles, hawks, and a flock of cormorants—birds so perpetually ravenous that any one of them will gulp down as many as 150 small fish per hour.

The Strait of Georgia

The most visually exciting of the Northwest's cruising grounds is unquestionably the 115-mile Strait of Georgia, separating the Canadian mainland from Vancouver Island. Protected by wooded mountains on both sides, the strait and its adjacent coves and estuaries boast such surprisingly balmy summer weather that local boatmen call the region the Banana Belt. The strait waters, contained in an enormous enclosed basin and baked by the sun, range upward from 60°—making them a full 15° warmer than the cool ocean currents of the adjacent Pacific.

The most interesting cruising in the strait—and the best anchorages—can be found among the deep indentations and ragged island groups along the eastern and northern shores. Only 50 miles north of Vancouver, the largest city in the Canadian West, is a mountain-lined fjord called Jervis Inlet, which cuts 40 miles inland. It terminates in a narrow offshoot, Princess Louisa Inlet *(right),* which one visitor described as "a magnified Yosemite carpeted by the sea." Because of gust winds and tidal currents, sailboats must normally travel both inlets under auxiliary; and all vessels must negotiate the mouth of Princess Louisa Inlet at slack water or face tide rips of up to nine knots.

Even more remote—and still largely untraveled—are the islands sprawled across the northern reaches of the strait. Hundreds of sheltered harbors, such as those in the fir-covered Octopus Islands *(pages 26-27),* offer not only seclusion but excellent crabbing and clamming, and some of the world's best salmon fishing. The area's prized Chinooks, or king salmon, routinely weigh in at 20 to 30 pounds apiece. But here, too, winds are flukey and tidal currents hazardous, and the lumber town and sport-fishing center of Campbell River on Vancouver Island is the only spot for serious provisioning.

The wake of a cruise boat momentarily disturbs the reflections of mile-high peaks on either side of Princess Louisa Inlet. An inland British Columbia marine park accessible only by boat, the inlet is five miles long, a half mile wide and so deep near shore that a boatman on deck can reach out and pluck oysters from the rocky walls.

Chatterbox Falls, at the northern end of Princess Louisa Inlet, cascades 120 feet from the precipice above. It is fed by snowmelt from the glaciated peaks of Canada's Pacific Coast range, which reach from 4,000 to 8,000 feet. The sloop is anchored over a sand bar near the falls, one of few spots in the inlet shallow enough for good holding ground.

A park float near Chatterbox Falls provides dock space for some of the thousand-odd pleasure boats that put in at Princess Louisa Inlet each year. Mooring space is also available just past the inlet's entrance, and early arrivals may drop anchor off Hamilton Island, halfway into the inlet, where the mountains give way to a small beach and visitors can bathe in water reaching 75° on a hot day.

A cedar pavilion, built in the style of local Sechelt Indian lodges, stands near Chatterbox Falls. It serves as a shelter and as a monument to the inlet's original owner, James MacDonald, who helped to make the land available to British Columbia as a park.

A particular hazard to Northwest navigators is the deadhead—a log like this one that has escaped from a tow and lies about, partially waterlogged, for months before sinking. This deadhead has been marked with a bright-orange pennant as a warning to boatmen.

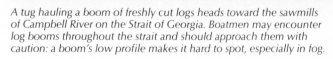

A tug hauling a boom of freshly cut logs heads toward the sawmills of Campbell River on the Strait of Georgia. Boatmen may encounter log booms throughout the strait and should approach them with caution: a boom's low profile makes it hard to spot, especially in fog.

A luxury cruising trawler rides peaceably at anchor in a perfect natural harbor formed by the tiny Octopus Islands, located just off the northeast corner of larger Quadra Island. The islands are uninhabited and provide excellent swimming, crabbing and fishing—not only for salmon but also for bottom fish such as snapper and cod. As in other sections fringing the strait, the narrow passages among the islands demand careful timing by approaching boatmen. During periods of peak ebb and flood tide, currents range from nine to 14 knots, generating impassable white-water rapids and whirlpools.

A family of harbor seals suns itself on the rocks of Octopus Island. Along with other fish-eating animals such as raccoons and bears, the seals are drawn to the area during the annual salmon run, when millions of coho, sockeye, Chinook, pink and chum salmon pass through on their way to spawning grounds in British Columbia. While the salmon are fair game to anyone with a fishing license, the seals enjoy the protection of strict Canadian hunting laws.

A humpback, or pink salmon, rests on the bottom of a British Columbia river after its long battle upstream to breed—and then die —in its native spawning grounds. Primarily a commercial salmon, it usually spawns in late summer, but only in odd-numbered years.

2 When the Portuguese explorer Juan Rodríguez Cabrillo first sailed up the California coast in 1542, he wrote in his journal: "There are mountains which reach to the heavens and the sea beats on them; sailing along close to land, it appears as though they would fall on us." Those of us who sail these waters today for pleasure no longer look upon the coastline with Cabrillo's uneasiness, but it is hard not to share his sense of awe. We Golden Staters think of the California shoreline—both the stretch within the United States and Baja California in Mexico—as one of the most scenic, most exciting cruising grounds in America, and marvelous to say, the season is almost year-round.

CALIFORNIA AND MEXICO'S BAJA

San Francisco Bay marks the effective northern limit of California cruising, since the seas above here are windy and rough, and harbors few. But if there has to be a limit, the bay makes a splendid one indeed. As Spanish seafarers noted with relief when they finally found the narrow passage of the Golden Gate two centuries after Cabrillo passed by, the waters inside are wide and reach far into the countryside. And, of course, few cities can match the charms of San Francisco. My husband Jack and I sometimes dock our 72-foot power cruiser, *Monsoon II,* at the marina east of the Presidio, within minutes of downtown, the maritime museum, Ghirardelli Square and the seafood eateries of Fisherman's Wharf.

Hundreds of pleasure boats and commercial craft ply the waters of San Francisco Bay, despite frequent fogs and brisk, erratic winds, which can sometimes be a real challenge. But when we head southeast from Golden Gate, prevailing northwesterlies make the going generally comfortable and fast. First stop is the compact little harbor of Monterey. The town seems to improve with every visit, reviving from its days as the ramshackle fishing village celebrated by John Steinbeck into a nicely restored version of its original self —California's provincial capital during Spanish rule.

From Monterey to San Simeon, 75 miles south, we churn past Seventeen Mile Drive and Cypress Point—a private world of golf courses and estates; past seductively beautiful but barely protected Carmel Bay and Point Lobos; and past miles of highlands, broken now and then by redwood-filled canyons. As we go, the lush greenery of the northern miles turns into tannish scrub. South of Point Arguello we have come to expect a marked change in weather: air temperatures are warmer, and the wind and seas calmer.

It's an easy 50-mile slide from Point Arguello to the lovely town of Santa Barbara, settled in 1782 as one of a string of Spanish garrisons along the coast. Santa Barbara is a logical take-off point for the northernmost of the eight Channel Islands that lie between here and San Diego. Sizable Santa Cruz, 22 miles southwest of the city, shares its 54,535 acres between a cattle ranch and a sheep ranch, and provides a choice of good anchorages on its northeastern shore. It also has a mammoth sea-level cave by Profile Point near the northwestern end of the island. On one recent visit, we set out in a dinghy to explore the cave. As we approached its 150-foot-high entrance, the sun picked up what looked like paint daubings on the rock face—copper, iron and zinc deposits mingling their corroded colors with brighter tints of sea lichen and the white streaks of guano left by cave-nesting birds. Cutting our motors just outside, we began to paddle stealthily into the darkness. Suddenly we heard a short, loud bark, and instantly the water was a maelstrom of snorting, splashing seals heading toward the mouth. When the exodus was over, one small seal pup remained clinging onto his rock shelf, either too afraid to move or too young to know better.

Santa Catalina and San Clemente mark the southern terminus of the Chan-

Some of San Francisco's 6,000 registered pleasure craft lie in slips at the St. Francis Yacht Club, a brief ride by bus and cable car from the posh high rises of Nob Hill in the distance.

nel group. While San Clemente is off-limits to all but the military, Santa Catalina is a popular stopover for mainlanders, and despite its proximity to the densely packed marinas of the Santa Barbara-to-San Diego area with their estimated population of 30,000 pleasure craft, it still manages to remain a marvelously unspoiled retreat. Grazing bison (descendants of a few imported for a 1920s movie), wild goats, Arabian stallions and wild boar are some of the animal life we have spotted here.

The complexion of California cruising changes once again in Mexican waters, south of San Diego. Slow economic development, sparse population and a simpler way of life are undeniably charming to outsiders. But for cruising folk, this rusticity can also bring problems. Fuel, drinking water, ice, and engine or rigging repairs are available in only a few places, and Baja *bodegas* and *super mercados* may not have one's favorite foods. Nevertheless, sailing down the Pacific coast of Baja and up into the blue brilliance of the Sea of Cortez (also called the Gulf of California) is for us one of the supreme experiences in boating—delightful from the first moments on. My journal of a recent cruise begins: "The first signs of dawn barely light the eastern skies as we set out past San Diego's Point Loma. We have plotted Isla Cedros, 320 miles below, as our first overnight stop, and by getting an early start we expect to make port before dark tomorrow. The *mañana* tempo is already beginning to work upon us. Porpoise frolic about our bows. Frequently a tiny canary-colored land bird flutters aboard to ride and rest awhile."

Reminiscing in the pilothouse next day, we recalled an earlier visit to Cedros when we were invited to a wedding and the whole town turned out for an all-day celebration. Cedros sits 40 miles west of huge Bahía Sebastián Vizcaíno and Scammon Lagoon, a shallow inner bay that is the winter nursery for thousands of gray whales from the Bering Sea. Farther south are Turtle Bay, the only truly sheltered harbor on this coast, generous-sized Bahía Magdalena and finally, at the tip of Baja, Cabo San Lucas.

When we first saw San Lucas in the 1940s it was just a remote village, beautiful to the eye and spirit, but significant only as the boundary between the Pacific and the Sea of Cortez. Now San Lucas has been "discovered," sport fishing for marlin and sailfish has been expanded to an industry, and a phalanx of luxury hotels has risen along the beach front. Similar changes have taken place around the cape in La Paz, which has grown into a bustling little city served by jets and ferries from the Mexican mainland. Its once-cobbled streets are now blacktopped, its ancient clanging windmills silenced. Still, the town remains lushly beautiful; seen from the harbor through palm and Indian laurel trees, it has an almost incandescent glow, which is accented by the fiery crimson of bougainvillea climbing up faded plaster walls.

After taking on supplies at La Paz, we can cruise on into the Sea of Cortez, putting in wherever wanderlust leads. The sea is a fantasy world for fishermen, a place where the angler becomes accustomed to pulling in fish of colors and shapes he never dreamed existed. The same is true of the bird life, vegetation and sea shells we have spotted along the peninsula's hundreds of miles of eastern shores.

At Mulegé, about midway up the Gulf, a narrow band of tropical greenery breaks into the long scroll painting of desert: here flows the Río Santa Rosalía, irrigating miles of date palms, mangoes, bananas and lemons. Just 12 miles farther up the coast at Punta Chivato is my favorite beachcombing spot; great mounds of shells, tossed up by southeastern storms, are on hand for the sorting. All along the way to Bahía de los Angeles and nearby Isla Ángel de la Guarda—the usual turn-around point—there is still a sense of serenity, of peacefulness and of original innocence. But go soon. As welcome as development may seem to the Mexicans, it will ultimately be bad news to the skin diver, the fisherman, the naturalist, and to the pleasure boatman who just wants to get off on his own.

by Carolyn West

A sun-drenched inlet on Bahía de LaPaz near the tip of Baja California offers an idyllic lunch stop for two cruising boats heading out into the Sea of Cortez. An impromptu feast of clams, rock oysters and the Mexican shellfish called hachas can be harvested in the shallows at the head of the cove to the right. The land is typically arid, with a sparse covering of thorny bur sage, prickly pear and agave, or century plant—which after years of quiescence sends up a single long stalk, as here, then flowers and dies.

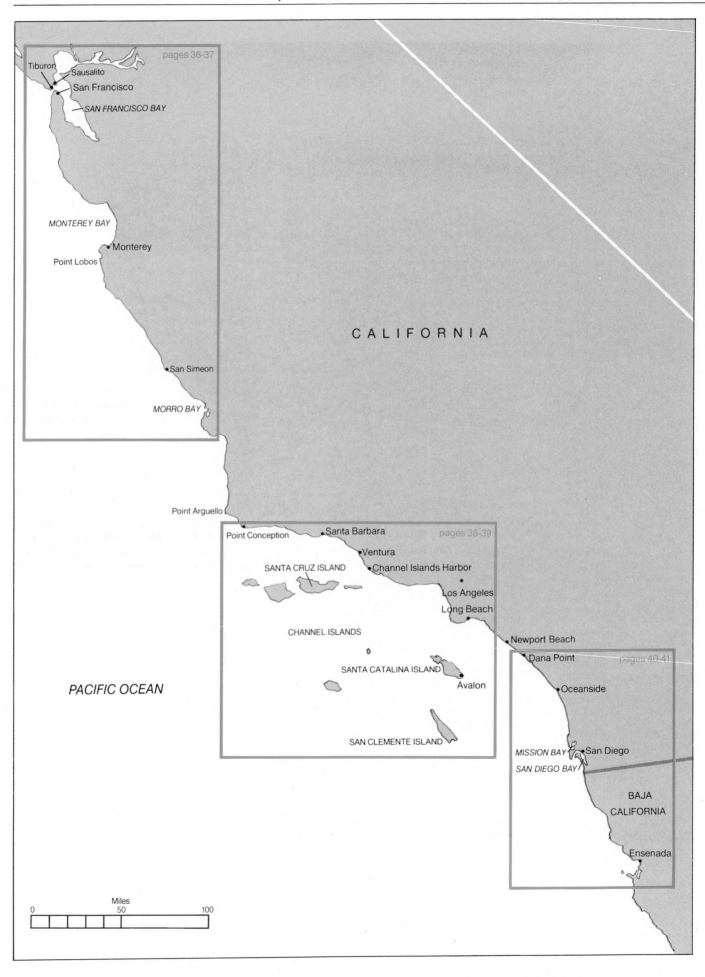

Tiburon
Sausalito
San Francisco
SAN FRANCISCO BAY

pages 36-37

MONTEREY BAY

•Monterey

Point Lobos

CALIFORNIA

•San Simeon

MORRO BAY

Point Arguello

Point Conception
Santa Barbara
pages 38-39
•Ventura
SANTA CRUZ ISLAND
•Channel Islands Harbor
Los Angeles
Long Beach

CHANNEL ISLANDS

Newport Beach
•Dana Point
pages 40-41

SANTA CATALINA ISLAND
Avalon

Oceanside

PACIFIC OCEAN

SAN CLEMENTE ISLAND

MISSION BAY
San Diego
SAN DIEGO BAY

BAJA
CALIFORNIA

Ensenada

Miles
0   50   100

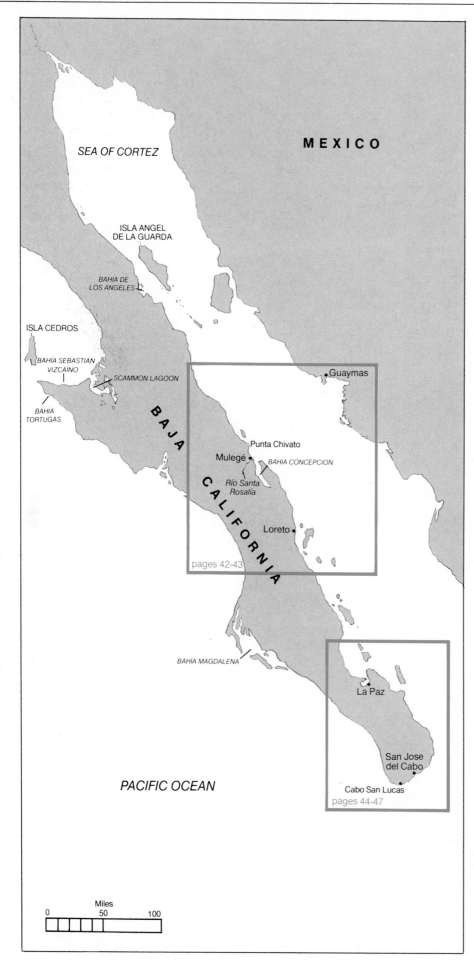

SEA OF CORTEZ

MEXICO

ISLA ANGEL
DE LA GUARDA

*BAHIA DE
LOS ANGELES*

ISLA CEDROS

*BAHIA SEBASTIAN
VIZCAINO*

SCAMMON LAGOON

•Guaymas

*BAHIA
TORTUGAS*

B A J A

C A L I F O R N I A

Punta Chivato

Mulegé•

BAHIA CONCEPCION

*Río Santa
Rosalía*

Loreto•

pages 42-43

BAHIA MAGDALENA

La Paz
•

San Jose
del Cabo
•

PACIFIC OCEAN

Cabo San Lucas•

pages 44-47

Miles

0   50   100

Two Californias

Each year some 30,000 yachtsmen set out to sample one or another of the five major cruising grounds between San Francisco and the tip of Baja California. The winds and waves along most of these cliff-bound areas demand stout boats and good seamanship, but other perils are few. And while the coast is poorly endowed with natural harbors, man-made facilities for pleasure craft are strategically located along the more populated stretches.

Along this edge of the continent the yachtsman will find an ever-changing panorama of great cities and soaring mountains, seaweed forests and water-carved pillars and arches. On the shores and in the waters live rare animals like the sea otter, and even rarer plants such as the Torrey pine, a survivor of the ice age.

From San Francisco to Point Arguello, the surf rages against narrow beaches and thrusting headlands. Cool winds snap in from the north, keeping air temperatures below 70° even in midsummer.

South of Point Conception, the climate is softer, the waters smoother. The mountains recede, leaving broad, sandy beaches, and the Channel Islands beckon boatmen to landfalls a short day's sail away.

Sunny skies and usually gentle winds make the coast from Dana Point to Ensenada—Baja California's only major Pacific port—a year-round cruising ground. Similar conditions apply clear down to the peninsula's tip—except for occasional summer gales—but Baja's parched west coast offers few cruising facilities.

Around the corner of Cabo San Lucas lies enchantment—the warm, generally calm, fish-filled Sea of Cortez. Formed when earthquakes split the land some 20 million years ago, this 600-mile lagoon is peppered with islands, fringed with natural harbors and weirdly beautiful desert uplands—enough for years of delightful exploration.

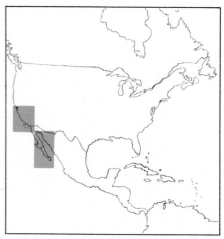

Winds and Weather

An even climate permits year-round cruising in almost all of the Pacific Coast from San Francisco south to Baja California. Daytime winter temperatures in the San Francisco area hover around 55°, and in summer reach the low 70s. South of Point Conception, temperatures average 10° warmer, winter and summer.

Prevailing winds blow in from the northwest, usually light in the morning but building to 15 to 20 knots in the afternoon. Precipitation is light; most rainfall occurs in winter. In late fall and winter, when atmospheric pressure rises in the desert plateau behind the Santa Ana Mountains, desiccating winds roll seaward across Southern California with gusts of 35 to 50 knots, and can carry offshore as far as 50 miles. Santa Ana winds arrive with little warning. A sailor who sees a dust cloud approaching rapidly from the east or northeast should strike sail immediately.

A more persistent hazard to California cruising is fog. Moist sea winds hit the cool California current offshore and condense. The resulting fogs seldom reach Baja California, nor do they penetrate the Sea of Cortez. Baja's annual rainfall averages 5.6 inches around La Paz. As July and August temperatures often reach 100°, the best cruising weather is March to June, when temperatures rise to 70° to 80°. The sea water seldom drops below 70°.

The breezes over the Sea of Cortez generally come from the northwest and blow at no more than five to 15 knots. Occasional winds of up to 25 knots can gust in at any time, however. And tropical storms, locally called *chubascos*, travel up the Sea of Cortez during the period from June through October.

Tides and Currents

Tides along the California coast are generally moderate, with a mean range of three to five feet. In the Sea of Cortez the tides are of little account, except at the far northern end. There the constricting effect of the shorelines is so pronounced that the tidal range in the extreme north can be as much as 20 to 30 feet.

Tidal currents also vary dramatically. At San Francisco, eddies around the Golden Gate Bridge piers can cause even large ships to sheer off course. Tidal currents are also strong in Morro Bay harbor and at the entrance to San Diego Bay. In La Paz harbor, winds and tides may create currents of up to six knots.

Pilotage

California coastal waters are generally deep and shoal-free even close inshore, though ground swell and breakers make a near approach to land unwise. A persistent problem all along the coast is the large kelp beds. Contact with kelp should be assiduously avoided. The tough strands will quickly entangle a propeller.

A different sort of hazard in some sections is the large amount of commercial shipping, especially around the Golden Gate and the Santa Barbara and San Pedro channels. Whenever possible, navigators should avoid charted vessel traffic lanes. In addition, sailors should steer clear of the offshore oil-drilling platforms in the Santa Barbara Channel and southeast of Long Beach.

In the Sea of Cortez, the sailor will find few navigation aids—and no Coast Guard. For these reasons alone, he must be extra cautious—particularly at night. During the day, however, visibility is so good that most piloting can be done by line of sight.

Harbors between San Francisco and Ensenada are deep. Where necessary, they have been dredged and protected with breakwaters. But in some harbors—Santa Cruz, Santa Barbara, Ventura, the Channel Islands Harbor and Oceanside—tidal currents may cause silting of access channels; boatmen should

enter with depth finder switched on. Call the harbor master on VHF Channel 16 for the latest conditions. Most anchorages in the Sea of Cortez are fairly deep, with sandy bottoms, providing good holding ground. Boats can sometimes anchor in the small coves at the tip of Baja, but there are no harbor facilities, and no protection from the summertime southeasterlies.

Boats and Special Equipment

Most Pacific-coast cruising occurs offshore and demands a sturdy, deep-draft vessel able to drive for long periods through head winds and heavy seas. Sailboats should be a minimum of 30 feet long, powerboats at least 35 feet. In the more sheltered Sea of Cortez, smaller craft, including trailered sail and power vessels as small as 20 feet long, can cruise safely. While there are few launching ramps along either shore, trailered boats can be launched from some beaches if the towing vehicle is equipped with four-wheel drive.

For a safe anchorage in the harbors along the California coast, boats should carry a standard burying-type anchor and as much as 300 feet of anchor rode. Experienced Pacific mariners bend on as much chain as they can comfortably handle to increase the anchor's holding power in the surges, swells and shifts of winds that commonly affect many anchorages.

A radio direction finder facilitates navigation in fogs. A boat equipped with a multiband radio receiver can pick up both the continuous National Weather Service broadcasts and local weather forecasts anywhere along the American coast. As local weather reports are broadcast in Spanish in Mexican waters, most skippers exchange weather information at 0800, 1200 and 1600 hours local time, using the 2638 kHz frequency.

Note that Baja California is still sparsely populated frontier country; if possible, boatmen are advised to cruise in company. Medical facilities are scarce; a cruising boat should carry a well-stocked first-aid kit that includes a medication recommended by a physician for intestinal upsets. Every boat should carry extra supplies of drinking water, food and fuel, and should be well stocked with spare parts. Fuel is sold by the liter. Mexican gasoline has a comparatively low octane rating; engine performance can be improved by mixing it half and half with aviation gasoline, obtainable at airstrips. Dockside gasoline pumps are rare; usually the fuel must be bought in towns, often directly from the drum—an operation that may require the yachtsman to furnish his own pump and hoses. All gasoline should be strained to remove sediment. Diesel fuel is usually of good quality but available at fewer places.

Wildlife

Among the hundreds of bird species that inhabit the California shore are petrels, cormorants, auklets and pigeon guillemots. Surfbirds include sandpipers, plover and curlews. Occasionally a blue heron or an egret is seen in a tidal marsh. Herds of seals, sea lions and sea otters thrive under government protection.

The coast has some famous migratory visitors. Pods of gray whales parade late every fall on their way to Scammon Lagoon on Baja's west coast, and convoy back north in spring. Swallows come every year on March 19 to San Juan Capistrano; in November emperor butterflies swarm to Pacific Grove.

In the Sea of Cortez, hunting has reduced the numbers of sea turtles, but the coastal bluffs and crags have large colonies of such sea birds as the brown pelican. Among the reptiles are assorted lizards, including the ferocious-looking but timid—and tasty—iguana.

Sports

The Pacific coastal waters off Southern California are unusually rich in fish of many types: tiny grunion which can be caught barehanded; sporty skipjack, bonito and albacore; giant striped marlin, swordfish, bluefin and yellowfin tuna. Yellowtail and kelp bass can be taken in kelp beds. In the Sea of Cortez, anglers can haul in blue and black marlin, 200-pound grouper, the 50- to 60-pound jewfish, striped corvina, roosterfish, amber jack and yellowtail. Among the shoreside mangroves are snook and snapper, also to be caught in lagoons and estuaries.

A license to catch salt-water fish off the U.S. coast is not necessary, but Mexico requires a permit from the government fishing commission offices in San Diego and San Pedro, at border crossing points or in most Baja ports. Mexico's license laws are strict; fishing without a permit draws a stiff fine. Surfing has long been a hallmark of Southern California, and the sun-warmed Sea of Cortez invites year-round swimming and scuba diving.

Regional Boating Regulations

A West Coast yachtsman visiting Mexico must first obtain several documents for the port captain at every port he enters: a crew list; a clearance document obtainable from any Mexican consulate; and a tourist card for each crew member, available, upon proof of U.S. citizenship, from the Mexican National Tourist Bureau. Before leaving a Mexican port, the boatman must secure a departure clearance from the port captain.

Entry permits, found at the border, are needed for vehicles, trailers and boats entering Mexico by land; passengers must have tourist cards. All vehicles should carry Mexican auto insurance (also obtainable at the border); Mexico accepts no other kind.

U.S. dollars are acceptable throughout most of Baja, but Mexican currency may be needed in smaller towns. Custom and courtesy require foreign craft to fly the Mexican flag while in Mexican waters. A returning boatman should, on arrival at the first U.S. port, phone the nearest U.S. customs office.

Major Provisioning Ports

Below is a list of ports on the California coast where cruising boats can take on stores. Each has fuel and is near marine-supply stores, markets, laundromats and repair yards, though few have extensive mooring facilities for visitors; visiting yachtsmen seeking accommodations should phone ahead to the harbor master.

San Francisco: One of the oldest, largest and most important of Pacific-coast ports. Space is provided for a few transient boats in its municipal small-craft harbor, with possible additional moorings available at Sausalito and Tiburon.

Monterey: The harbor here offers a few berths at the well-protected marina, and room to anchor just inside the outer breakwater.

Morro Bay: An all-weather, landlocked harbor midway between San Francisco and Los Angeles.

Channel Islands Harbor: A mainland port close to the Channel Islands. The harbor can accommodate 1,495 boats in all, some of them transients.

Los Angeles/Long Beach: One of the largest man-made harbors in the world, with a nine-mile-long stone breakwater. Alamitos Bay at the eastern end has 2,500 feet of mooring space for transients. The area serves boats cruising to Santa Catalina.

San Diego: A large natural harbor that is home port to 4,600 pleasure boats and the jumping-off point for the long haul around Baja peninsula.

La Paz: The major provisioning center on the western shore of the Sea of Cortez. It has fishing boats for charter, and a shipyard.

Guaymas: A town on the east shore of the Sea of Cortez. It has complete services for boatmen, several good hotels and charter fishing.

Coast Guard Stations

Two Coast Guard districts patrol the California coast. The 12th has headquarters in San Francisco, and operates as far south as Morro Bay with four stations. The 11th, in Long Beach, has seven stations. The Coast Guard maintains search-and-rescue stations at San Diego, Los Angeles and San Francisco.

Charts and Publications

The cruising area from San Francisco south to San Diego is covered by U.S. National Ocean Survey charts 18022, 18680, 18700, 18720 and 18740, Volume III of the light lists, the West Coast tide tables and the *Coast Pilot 7*. For local charts check the National Ocean Survey *Nautical Chart Catalog 2*. For sailing in the Sea of Cortez, bring *Sailing Directions No. 153* and charts, published by the U.S. Department of Defense Hydrographic Center. Charts 18000, 21011 and 21014 cover the west coast of Baja. Charts 21014 and 21008 cover the Sea of Cortez. Local charts are listed in the Defense Mapping Agency's *Catalog of Nautical Charts, Region 2*. Appropriate government agencies are:

National Ocean Survey
Distribution Division, C44
6501 Lafayette Avenue
Riverdale, Maryland 20840

Defense Mapping Agency Depot
5801 Tabor Avenue
Philadelphia, Pennsylvania 19120

Useful piloting and cruising guides for this area include:

Berssen, Capt. William, USCGR (Ret.), *Pacific Boating Almanac, Northern California and Nevada Edition*. Ventura, Calif.: William Berssen Publications.
Pacific Boating Almanac, Southern California, Arizona, Baja Edition. Ventura, Calif.: William Berssen Publications.
Crawford, Capt. William P., *Sea Marine Atlas, Southern California*. Newport Beach, Calif.: Sea Publications, Inc.
Jones, Vern, and Louis Gerlinger, *Baja California Cruising Notes*. San Diego, Calif.: SeaBreez Publications.
Lewis, Leland R., and Peter E. Ebeling:
Baja Sea Guide. Newport Beach, Calif.: Sea Publications, Inc.
Sea Guide, Southern California. Newport Beach, Calif.: Sea Publications, Inc.
West, Carolyn and Jack, *Cruising the Pacific Coast, Acapulco to Skagway*. Newport Beach, Calif.: Sea Publications, Inc.

The Central Shoreline

Nowhere is the coast of California more spectacular—and also poorer in refuges for yachtsmen—than along the 188-mile sweep from San Francisco south to Morro Bay. Sheer sandstone cliffs and mountain ramparts abut narrow beaches constantly bombarded by the Pacific surf.

At the southern end of 20-mile-wide Monterey Bay is the largest of the few existing anchorages, a snug harbor for some 500 fishing and pleasure craft. A skipper can anchor behind the breakwater or tie up at the marina and visit Cannery Row, celebrated in John Steinbeck's novel of the same name. Or he can take a 17-mile limousine tour of the Monterey Peninsula through groves of pine and the unique, wind-twisted Monterey cypress.

Carmel Bay on the peninsula's south shore offers a tight anchorage among rocky islets in the lee of famed Pebble Beach Golf Course. Visitors are permitted to play on this difficult scenic course, but should make advance reservations.

For 95 miles below Carmel there are only partially sheltered anchorages like San Simeon—a possible stopover for visiting William Randolph Hearst's 100-room castle. Some 25 miles farther south is the nearly landlocked harbor of Morro Bay, with some of the coast's best clamming, crabbing and sport fishing.

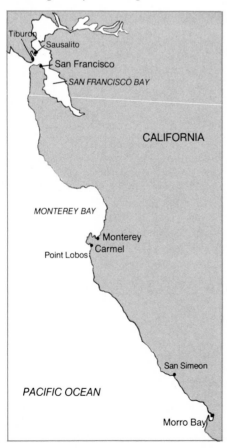

At the start of a day's passage, a cruising boat stands out across Morro Bay, heading past white beaches that sweep away from 576-foot-high Morro Rock and into the narrow dog-leg channel that leads to the sea. Outside the channel, the bay shoals in places from 11 feet down to two feet; but the surrounding waters swirl with albacore, salt-water salmon and cod. A large fishing complex at the head of the bay offers moorings, fuel, several fine restaurants and bicycle rentals for pedaling through the 6,000 acres of nearby state parklands.

Carmel's premier show place, an old Spanish mission with a Moorish bell tower and gardens of poppy and bougainvillea, exemplifies the vintage charm of the colonial sites that dot the Monterey area. Founded in 1770, the mission is one of nine that were set up by a slight, five-foot-two Franciscan, the indefatigable Father Junípero Serra. He started the mission as a log-cabin complex, and it was expanded seven times; the present basilica dates from 1797. The mission can be visited daily from 9:30 a.m. to 5:30 p.m.

Point Lobos, at the southern tip of Carmel Bay, emerges from a light morning mist, common in this area during the summer. The point is a state park with rocky headlands abounding in sea otters, seals and sea lions —which the Spanish called sea wolves, or "lobos," thus giving the point its name. In the background are the white spires of a monastery built in 1931 for Carmelite nuns.

Dank fog engulfs Monterey's Cannery Row, a string of ramshackle fish-processing plants built in the early 1900s. During 1941 and 1942, the canneries tinned 250,000 tons of sardines; but the fish mysteriously vanished, and by 1947 the industry had failed. Restaurants, shops and art galleries now occupy some of the buildings and earn more than the fish canneries ever did.

The Channel Islands

Stretched out for 130 miles off the coast of California is a string of eight isolated eminences called the Channel Islands. Beautiful to look at and notched with numerous anchorages, they are great favorites with cruising yachtsmen—in spite of frequent morning and evening fogs, and 20-knot crosswinds that intrude on the passage from the mainland.

Though some of the islands have been settled for centuries, deer, elk, bison and wild boar also occupy the land, as do seals, sea lions and the largest colony of sea elephants in the United States. Gray whales and porpoises frequent the clear waters, and sea birds crowd the cliffs. Spring rains bring explosions of wild flowers. On three of the islands, giant coreopsis grow up to eight feet tall, their yellow mass of blooms visible for 10 miles at sea.

The three seawardmost islands, San Miguel, San Nicolas and San Clemente, are military reservations; civilian visitors may anchor but may not come ashore. Anacapa and Santa Barbara are a joint national monument, open to day visits or camping. But during the busy summer season yachtsmen should check first with the U.S. Park Service to see if camping space is available. And they should bring their own supplies, including fresh water.

Voyagers wishing to explore privately owned Santa Rosa and Santa Cruz must obtain landing permits in advance.

Santa Catalina, most popular of the islands, is owned in the main by the Wrigley chewing-gum family. But its principal yacht basin is open to unrestricted landing, and the basin's surrounding community of Avalon is public and available to all comers.

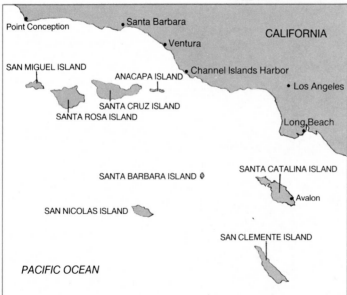

Two California gray whales surface on their way to summer feeding grounds in the Bering Sea. Thousands of these great creatures pass the Channel Islands each year on their 8,000-mile round trip from Baja California, where couples mate and cows give birth.

A stout cruising sloop lies at anchor in one of several scenic coves on 54,535-acre Santa Cruz, largest of the islands and the private preserve of two cattle-and-sheep-ranching firms. Santa Cruz briefly served Mexico as a penal colony in the 19th Century, and was later a rendezvous for smugglers and bootleggers. Today visitors can go ashore with the owners' permission.

On a perfect sailing day, only about 40 craft remain tethered among the 95 private moorings in Santa Catalina's main harbor of Avalon. The white building at upper right, the Avalon Casino, was opened in 1929 as a dance pavilion and still attracts the big-name musicians. During the summer, it is floodlit at night and serves as a brilliant landmark for sailors heading over from mainland yachting centers such as Newport Beach.

The Border Region

Brisk and usually dependable breezes, limpid waters, spectacular scenery and a sunny subtropical climate make the coast from Los Angeles to Ensenada a tempting year-round cruising ground. Its only shortcoming is the one besetting all California cruising—a lack of natural sheltered anchorages. Between San Diego and Newport Beach (just below Los Angeles) there is no natural all-weather harbor.

However, the situation has been alleviated by the construction of some small-craft ports. Dana Point Harbor, once no more than a rough dent in the coast 13 miles south of Newport Beach, was transformed in 1970 by the building of jetties into a snug mooring site for 2,000 boats. Another 20 miles to the south, man-made Oceanside Harbor was opened in 1963 to accommodate 800 vessels.

The one great natural harbor in the region is San Diego Bay, which offers not only berths for 4,600 pleasure boats but also room enough for day-long sailing excursions. Just to the north is Mission Bay Park, a 2,000-acre marine complex with 2,000 boat slips, designated water-skiing areas and an aquatic circus as fascinating as Florida's more famed Marineland.

Below San Diego, however, along the whole 769-mile stretch of Mexico's Baja California, there is only one protected spot where a yachtsman can buy provisions and go ashore to relax amid civilized surroundings. This is Ensenada, 55 miles below the border. Ensenada is filled with lively restaurants and nightclubs, and although parts of the town are stained by the commercial flotsam that washes up near almost any border area, there is the compensating attraction of duty-free stores with their bargains in watches, cameras, Mexican clothing and leather goods.

San Diego Bay, one of the Pacific coast's finest natural harbors, measures four miles across, from the steep-roofed San Diego Yacht Club (foreground) to the city's high-rise office buildings. Dredging has enlarged the 14-mile-long bay to 25 square miles of navigable waters for the port's 4,250 or so small craft. Lying between the yacht club and the main bay is palm-fringed Shelter Island, one of two islands that were built with the spoil from the dredging.

The wild grandeur of the Torrey Pines bluffs, just 15 miles north of San Diego, is typical of scenery along much of the Southern California coast. The sandstone sea walls, towering 300 feet from their windswept summits down to the narrow beaches, are named for an ancient species of pine unique to the area. The trees grow in scattered groves on the tops of the cliffs, and are grotesquely gnarled and splayed from the constant winds and the withering salt sea spray.

A cluster of cruising boats lies anchored at Ensenada, Mexico's port of entry for the Pacific coast of Baja California. Popular with adventurous California yachtsmen on long weekend cruises, this busy seaport plays host each April to some 500 finishers in the Newport Beach-to-Ensenada ocean race.

A sloop at anchor on Bahía Concepción, a finger of the Sea of Cortez,
lies just a short dinghy ride from the palm-leaf pavilions built by the
Mexican government to shade visitors from the sun. Twenty-two miles
long but only five miles across at its widest point, Concepción lures a
rich concentration of fish from the surrounding waters. Fishermen
consistently reel in succulent dorado, sierra and cabrilla; a prize
catch may be a baya grouper, which can weigh 230 pounds. On the
beach, a deft forager using only his bare hands can scoop up butter
clams by the fistful or pluck trapped fish from the tidal pools.

The Sea of Cortez

Wedged between the peninsula of Baja California and the Mexican mainland, the Sea of Cortez is difficult for U.S. boatmen to reach, a factor that has helped to keep it one of the world's most beautiful places to cruise. There are three ways—all rather difficult—for a sailor to get to this choice region, whose central sector is shown here. He can run down the long Pacific coast of Baja and round the cape to the sea. He can drive or fly directly to one of Baja's east-coast ports—La Paz, Loreto, Mulegé—to charter a boat with a Mexican captain and crew. Or he can trailer his boat, either down Baja's Transpeninsula Highway or down the east shore to the fishing-and-resort port of Guaymas.

From June through mid-September, the Sea of Cortez can be uncomfortably hot. But throughout the rest of the year—save for an occasional norther that brings in sweater weather—there is no better climate: daytime air temperatures hover in the 80s, and evenings are cool for sleeping. The water stays an even 70 to 75°.

The sea itself is uncommonly rich in nutrients that feed a staggering 658 species of fish, some of which travel in schools of almost unbelievable size. It is not uncommon to see tiny forage fish in a horde 10 miles long and a half mile wide being pursued by ranks of game fish in equal numbers. Manta rays 15 to 24 feet across leap through the water's surface. Overhead the sky teems with hungry sea birds—pelicans, frigates, terns and boobies.

The Baja shoreline can also be bounteous; the pale beaches yield bushels of shellfish, and the bare, austere mountain ranges are surprisingly full of wildlife —mountain lion, bighorn sheep, deer, bobcat, dove and quail. The towns on shore, though few and relatively far between, retain the sleepy engaging quality that elsewhere—in too much of modern Mexico—exists only in travel folders.

A cruising boat's crew lolls under a cockpit awning in the landlocked lagoon of Puerto Escondido, or "Hidden Harbor." At the lagoon's narrow entrance, there are currents of up to four knots. Once on the lagoon, however, fishermen can troll for game fish, including black snook, snappers and ladyfish.

An employee of the Serenidad Hotel at Mulegé roasts a pig for the regular Saturday-night fiesta. Visiting yachtsmen can, for a reasonable dinner price, join the feast, which is held outdoors under the date palms that give Mulegé much of its income. Date trees planted by Jesuit missionaries in 1705 still thrive—yielding a cash crop—along the banks of the Río Santa Rosalía, one of the few rivers in all of Baja California.

Two stone crosses rise above seaward-jutting Punta Santa Cruz, where Baja's first explorers, members of a 16th Century Spanish expedition, are said to have landed. The tile-roofed buildings in the background are part of Rancho Las Cruces, once a fruit-tree plantation but now a private club for affluent sport fishermen. A small breakwater provides some shelter for the club's boats but no room for visitors, who must anchor offshore.

A fishing party hauls in a prized dorado near Cabo San Lucas. Among the fiercest of game fish, a mature dorado, when hooked, sometimes hurls its 50- to 75-pound body 15 feet in the air, then swims so furiously an angler using light tackle may need two hours to boat his catch. While battling, the fish changes colors—up to 11 different hues—in an instinctive, chameleon-like effort to confuse pursuers and evade capture.

Its spinnaker tugging in a stiff westerly, a sloop runs past the granite headlands of Cabo San Lucas at the tip of Baja in a majestic seascape of long swells set against dramatic rock formations ashore. Capitalizing on this grandeur, a string of luxury hotels has gone up since the 1950s along the 20 miles of coastline from the cape toward San José del Cabo to the east. In calm weather, visiting yachtsmen can anchor along the shore, check into a hotel (most require reservations), wash off the salt in an onyx-lined bath, sip drinks on a flowered veranda and dine at a table overlooking the rolling surf.

The Cape

The richest fishing ground in all the Sea of Cortez lies at the sea's entrance just east of Cabo San Lucas at the very tip of Baja California. Here fleets of big game fish feed just offshore—marlin, swordfish, sailfish, yellowfin tuna. With them are schools of cabrilla, bonito, roosterfish and the delicious dorado *(opposite, below)*. The marlin are the largest; mature specimens weigh up to 100 pounds.

This profusion of game fish supports a booming charter-boat fleet serving sportsmen who fly down from the mainland or sail down on their own cruising craft. Charter boats are based in each resort anchorage along the south and southeast coast from Cabo San Lucas to La Paz. The best harbor is at La Paz, a charming old Spanish town with tree-lined streets and flower-rimmed patios. Entrance to the anchorage, which can accommodate as many as 50 pleasure boats, leads past shifting sand bars along a well-marked channel. Other southern Baja anchorages are small. And though a few boats can often find space there, these harbors are used mainly by local fishermen and can be uncomfortable in southerly winds.

The land around La Paz and much of the cape's southern coastline is somewhat greener than in the countryside farther north. Rainfall is heavier in the south, and there are irrigated truck farms and orchards. Boatmen should note, however, that strong southeasterlies may bluster in during the summer and early fall, causing rougher seas than in the protected northern reaches of the Sea of Cortez. And during the same seasons small localized hurricanes, called *chubascos,* may· hit the area with damaging 50- to 60-knot gusts and very high waves.

Rancho Las Cruces

La Paz

SEA OF CORTEZ

BAJA CALIFORNIA

PACIFIC OCEAN

San José del Cabo

Cabo San Lucas

A tropical sun sets behind Cabo San Lucas, burnishing the western
sky for a brilliant moment. The two conical rocks at the cape's tip,
called Los Frailes, or "The Friars," mark both the end of Baja California
and the theoretical line dividing the Sea of Cortez from the Pacific.

3 Anyone adventurous enough to have paddled, poled, rafted, sailed or powered his way up or down one of America's hundreds of navigable rivers knows how fascinating and exhilarating the experience can be. Mark Twain, a first-rate river pilot in his youth, summed it up when he called the mighty Mississippi "a wonderful book [with] a new story to tell every day...never a page that was void of interest, never one that you could leave unread without loss, never one that you would want to skip, thinking you could find higher enjoyment in some other thing." Always moving, always alive, busily coming from someplace and bound for another, these rivers offer an

CRUISING RIVERS OF AMERICA

eternal invitation to the pleasure-boater to venture around the next bend.

Though perhaps a dozen of America's greatest streams have been cruised for centuries, the nation's present wealth of navigable courses for pleasure boats is relatively new, the result of four decades of dredging, dam building and continuing maintenance by the U.S. Army Corps of Engineers. The total length of improved river channels in the United States is now more than 30,000 miles, and there are few Americans who do not live within an easy day's drive of one or more such waterways. Further, the federally sponsored Wild and Scenic Rivers Act, created in 1968, promises to set aside systematically additional inland waterways and to preserve areas of natural and uncluttered beauty for recreational boating.

Within this vast network a mariner will find an almost limitless variety: fast-flowing rivers like the central and lower Mississippi; languid, unhurried rivers like the St. Johns; rivers such as the Hudson, whose single channel is bracketed by high rocky ramparts; and rivers like the Sacramento, whose delta is a complex water web entangling low, grassy islets. There are rivers that turn into lakes; the fast-flowing Missouri does so at a number of man-made dams —Fort Peck Lake, Lake Sakakawea, Lake Oahe, and Lewis and Clark Lake, among them. And there are lakes that turn into rivers, e.g., Lake Ontario where it pinches into the St. Lawrence. There are stretches of river so little trafficked that a boatman can almost imagine himself a frontier explorer—the canyons of the upper Missouri (opposite) are like that. And there are rivers, like the Ohio and the Tennessee, whose shores are so packed with history and legend that gliding through them is like traveling in a time machine.

A small shallow-draft cabin cruiser or a houseboat are by all odds the craft most adaptable to river travel. But almost any vessel will suffice. American boatmen glide down the nation's waterways in everything from life rafts to canal boats to canoes to converted freight barges. Thus, in areas where camping facilities and launching ramps are available at river's edge, the boatman can assume the guise of a modern Huck Finn, floating light and easy in an outboard runabout, say, and savoring his watery world just as well as—if not better than—his more posh brethren on larger, faster craft. Even an auxiliary sailboat will do nicely in some limited areas, like the wide, deep reaches of the lower Hudson and the California Delta.

Whatever the choice, the boatman will discover a very special kind of cruising on the rivers—one with its own special variety of delights and challenges. On the lower Mississippi, for example, he will proceed along a winding, unmarked channel in a 15-mile-wide flood plain—the so-called meander belt, through which the river shifts its course from week to week and from day to day. And he will quickly learn what young Mark Twain found out as an apprentice pilot: navigating among the bends and bars and snags and currents of a river can demand skills that are every bit as precise as those required on any body of salt water.

A powerboat with a skier in tow cuts across six-mile-long Holter Lake in Montana—one of five small-craft cruising grounds that have been created by dams along the upper Missouri.

Six of the Best

Of the great diversity of navigable rivers within the continental United States, the six systems shown at right represent a sampling of the finest for inland cruising. Like all of the nation's rivers, they course through one or another of four enormous drainage areas: west from the snowy crests of the Rocky Mountains toward the Pacific; south from the eastern slopes of the Rockies and western slopes of the Appalachians through broad agricultural heartland to the Gulf of Mexico; east from the Appalachians through the coastal plain into the Atlantic; or east from the Great Lakes to the St. Lawrence River. Together, they offer a continent's worth of cruising diversity and excitement.

The largest of these systems, the Mississippi and its tributaries, runs through the American midland. The principal section open to cruising boats—outlined in blue and described on pages 58-59—is the 1,832-mile stretch from the Gulf of Mexico north to Minneapolis-St. Paul. Boats with shallow draft can run another 513 miles north, after passing through the St. Anthony Falls locks and dams. The Mississippi's largest tributary, the Missouri, is navigable upstream for 754 miles to Ponca State Park, Nebraska. Above Ponca, however, cruising is restricted to craft that can be trailered to a broken chain of lakes extending into Montana.

The Mississippi's second largest tributary is the Ohio, which is navigable for its entire 981-mile length through a series of 21 locks and dams. Some seven other satellite rivers and streams add another 1,000 miles of accessible water routes.

Along the Atlantic coast, the most popular and longest fresh-water artery is the Hudson and its connecting channels. Together they carry cruisers 434 miles north from New York Harbor via Lake Champlain to the St. Lawrence, and 357 miles west along the New York State Barge Canal from Troy to Lake Erie.

On the continent's western slopes, the Colorado has been impounded into a series of man-made lakes. There are four major lakes, each partly enclosed by lofty canyons. Distinctly different in character are the California Delta rivers, including the Sacramento and San Joaquin, which converge to form the great slough-laced delta behind San Francisco Bay.

The St. Johns River in Florida originates in marshlands in Indian River County, barely 20 feet above sea level. More like a continuous lagoon than a river, it meanders more than 280 miles to Jacksonville and the Atlantic.

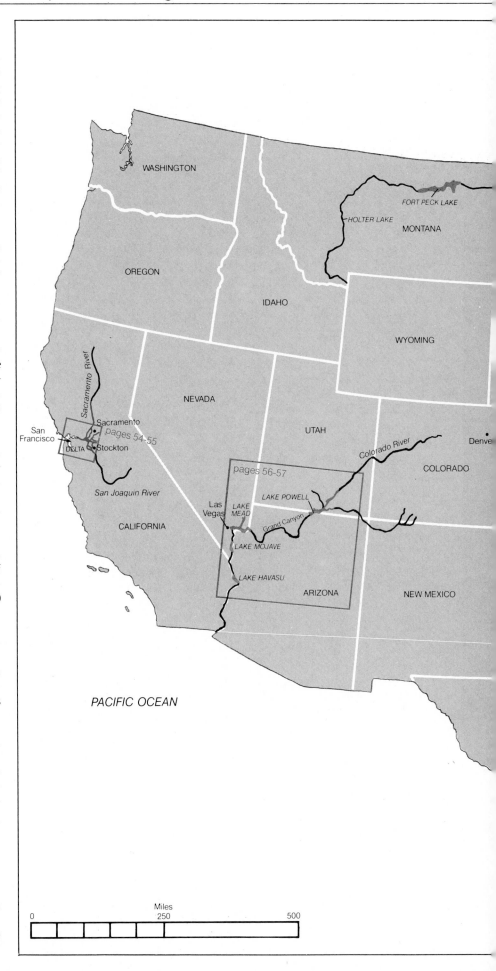

NORTH DAKOTA

LAKE SAKAKAWEA

MINNESOTA

SOUTH DAKOTA

LAKE OAHE

Minneapolis • St. Paul

pages 58-59

WISCONSIN

MICHIGAN

LEWIS AND CLARK LAKE

• Sioux City

IOWA

ILLINOIS

Chicago •

NEBRASKA

pages 60-61

St. Louis •

MISSOURI

Louisville •

INDIANA

Cincinnati •

OHIO

Ohio River

WEST
VIRGINIA

KANSAS

Cairo •

KENTUCKY

LAKE BARKLEY

KENTUCKY LAKE

Paducah •

Nashville •

Cumberland River

• Knoxville

VIRGINIA

NORTH
CAROLINA

OKLAHOMA

ARKANSAS

TENNESSEE

Chattanooga •

Tennessee River

SOUTH
CAROLINA

ATLANTIC OCEAN

TEXAS

MISSISSIPPI

ALABAMA

GEORGIA

LOUISIANA

• Natchez

Mississippi River

pages 64-65

Jacksonville •

St. Johns River

LAKE GEORGE

New Orleans •

Sanford •

FLORIDA

VERMONT

MAINE

pages 62-63

LAKE CHAMPLAIN

NEW HAMPSHIRE

Troy •

Albany •

MASSACHUSETTS

Buffalo •

New York State
Barge Canal

NEW
YORK

Hudson River

RHODE ISLAND

CONNECTICUT

Allegheny River

PENNSYLVANIA

Pittsburg •

Monongahela River

New York City •

NEW JERSEY

DELAWARE

MARYLAND

Mississippi River

Illinois River

Missouri River

Favored Cruising Waters

Shallow or Obstructed Waters

Winds and Weather

A boatman cruising a river must bear in mind that he is moving primarily in a land-bound environment, where wind direction and strength are dramatically influenced by surrounding terrain. The upper Hudson, for instance, cuts a narrow path beneath rolling, wooded hills, and its winds average a leisurely 8.8 miles per hour over the year. But on the Arizona desert, where intense heat creates great convection currents, spring winds average 15 to 20 miles per hour, and storms whip over the Colorado River's lakes at 60 miles per hour.

Seasonal changes in weather can bring major fluctuations in water level. The mighty Mississippi, fed by some 20 major tributaries and hundreds of lesser streams that pour into it from 31 states, rises by as much as 50 feet from snow runoff between January and June. Even the small sloughs of the California Delta rise as much as 10 to 13 feet in spring.

Seasonal temperature changes are also a key factor on rivers. On the Hudson, Ohio, upper and middle Mississippi, and Colorado, winter temperatures in the 20s and below bring ice, which makes wet storage very risky and the rivers unnavigable for small craft from December into February. Florida's St. Johns and other Southern rivers, including the lower Mississippi, are navigable by pleasure craft in all seasons; but mariners should keep in touch with weather developments in September and October, the season when hurricanes strike.

Tides and Currents

The distance that ocean tides travel up a river from the coast depends upon the tidal range, the strength of the river's current and the incline of the river bed. The Sacramento and San Joaquin rivers, whose mouths lie 20 miles from the open Pacific, are affected by tides for only 15 miles or so upstream. But the Hudson is tidal for 126 miles upstream to Albany. The flat, meandering St. Johns River is a mixture of fresh and salt water for much of its length, and tidal rise and fall is negligible.

Fresh-water currents, generated by the rivers themselves, are a complex problem—and opportunity—for the boatman. Current velocity depends upon the depth of the water and the degree of bend in the river. Boats traveling downstream will make the best time by following the deepest—hence fastest—part of the channel. Boats going against the current will meet the least resistance over the shallower lanes of the river—usually closer to shore and near the inside bank at bends—though navigating in this manner requires close attention to water depths. Where a river moves from a narrow passage to a relatively wide one or where it is dammed by locks, the current will diminish.

Pilotage

The river pilot must be on constant lookout for hazards too new or transitory to appear on charts or to be buoyed. A river erodes and holds in suspension great quantities of sediment, dumping some each time it encounters an impediment; shoals constantly build along shallow banks and inside bends. A skipper whose boat draws close to the charted depths should proceed cautiously and seek local information. If there is no depth finder on board, he should be sure to watch the boat's wake: a wake becomes sharply peaked and its regular pattern is broken on entering shallow water.

Floating debris, especially after spring flooding or a heavy rainfall, is a hazard on rivers, requiring a steady eye ahead by the skipper. Often it is a good idea to post a lookout on the bow.

Traversing locks and passing under bridges and other overhead obstructions present further obstacles for the pilot. Vertical clearances at mean high water of fixed bridges, power cables and the like are generally marked on river charts; in some rivers clearance is prohibitively low for boats with fixed masts—15½ feet on the New York State Barge Canal System, for example.

When approaching a lock or drawbridge, the boatman must signal by radio or the prescribed horn signal, or by a small-craft signal device on the lock wall, and then await the answering signal—meanwhile keeping clear of boats holding priority (see the Regional Boating Regulations section opposite). Upon entering a lock the boat should be made fast to the snubbing posts with bow and stern lines. All flames aboard must be extinguished.

Other problems are particular to some rivers. Crossing the path of one of the cable-drawn ferries in the California Delta, a skipper must wait until the ferry reaches the shore and the cable slackens sufficiently to permit passage. The Mississippi has submerged rock breakwaters and is troubled with a phenomenon known as flocculation—the existence of masses of jellied muck from 10 to 15 feet deep carried by the current. Floccules can clog water strainers and damage strut bearings and shafts.

Boats and Special Equipment

On slow-moving, shallow rivers, and wherever winds are fluky and distances short between stopovers, a houseboat is probably the best choice for cruising; however, it must have sufficient horsepower to cope with the currents likely to be met en route. Auxiliary sailboats will find good cruising in the broad, straight lower reaches of some large rivers, but opportunities to sail diminish in the narrower parts upstream. Trailer boats offer a wide range of cruising choices; but since state highway laws vary, skippers should inquire ahead.

A boatman cruising the Mississippi should have a radio to check on weather and on up-to-date shoaling information. A two-way radio is also very useful (but not essential) for communicating with bridge and lock operators. A good burying anchor is one of the best for muddy bottoms; on the deep Colorado River lakes, extra line will serve for hitching up to a tree or rock pinnacle on shore. For canal and lock cruising, dock lines 50 feet long and plenty of fenders are essential.

Wildlife

Even heavily trafficked rivers offer a prodigious variety of wildlife. The Mississippi flyway is a funnel for such species of birds as canvasback ducks and Canada geese. The California Delta is a stopping place for, among others, the green-winged teal and whistling swan, on the Pacific flyway. The St. Johns is home to tropical creatures—manatee, turtles and chameleons; the Cumberland and Tennessee have a mixed bag that includes deer, mink and wild turkey. And though most of the desert wildlife around Lake Powell is out of the boatman's line of vision, coyotes can be heard to howl in the night from the canyon rims.

Sports

Except where industrial waste causes pollution, rivers are natural fishing grounds. A boatman with a rod and reel or a net can find some ubiquitous species—most notably bass—in practically all of them. Shad run upstream seasonally on estuarial rivers, and shellfish, such as crab, can be found in some of them. An angler may well find the most prolific sport fishing of all on the dammed lakes, such as Powell, Barkley and Kentucky, which the various state agencies stock annually. Fishing licenses can be obtained from the departments of fish and wildlife for the states through which the river flows.

Rivers also provide natural sites for campers, and many states and federal agencies maintain parks near wooded riverbanks.

Regional Boating Regulations

The Rules of the Road under which boats operate on U.S. rivers vary slightly from system to system. U.S. Coast Guard Inland Rules govern rivers that empty into the Pacific and Atlantic (including the Mississippi Delta and Lake Pontchartrain). A second set, the Western Rivers Rules, apply to rivers feeding into the Mississippi—i.e., virtually every river between the Rockies and the Ohio headwaters. (An unusual feature of the Western Rivers Rules gives right of way to boats going downstream; Inland Rules make no such distinction.)

In addition, state and local authorities may set stricter limits than federal ones on speed, water pollution, etc. And the Army Corps of Engineers has its own priority system for boats using its lock facilities during periods of heavy traffic: government vessels go first, followed by commercial passenger boats, commercial freight and fishing boats; pleasure boats are last.

Major Provisioning Ports

The ports below—listed by river, and from west to east—are not necessarily the rivers' largest cities; they are places where, in addition to food and mooring facilities, a boatman can find fuel, repairs and other services for the needs of pleasure craft.

> **San Joaquin River:** Stockton—one of the largest seaports on the West Coast and a good entry point into the California Delta.
> **Colorado River:** Wahweap—not a port, but a marina, five miles north of Glen Canyon Dam, on Lake Powell. Wahweap has launching ramps and cruising craft for rent.
> **Mississippi River:** Portage des Sioux—on the Missouri shore about 30 miles upstream from St. Louis, and a major pleasure-boating center for the middle Mississippi. Other small-craft ports include Red Wing on the Minnesota shore of the upper river and Natchez on the lower river.
> **Ohio River:** Louisville—some distance below the commercial ports of Pittsburgh and Cincinnati. Other ports in the Ohio River basin include Paducah, Nashville on the Cumberland, and Chattanooga on the Tennessee.
> **Hudson River:** Nyack—25 miles upstream from New York City. Schuylerville—20 miles north of Albany, within a day's run of Lake Champlain.
> **St. Johns River:** Jacksonville—Florida's second largest commercial seaport, 21 miles inland.

Coast Guard and Other Rescue Stations

Search and rescue operations on U.S. rivers are conducted by various federal, state and local agencies.

The Sacramento and San Joaquin rivers are supervised by a Coast Guard station based at Rio Vista, California. The Colorado River lakes are assigned to the National Park Service and local county officials. The Mississippi River from the Gulf to Baton Rouge comes under the aegis of the Eighth Coast Guard District,

with headquarters in New Orleans. From Baton Rouge all the way to Minneapolis the Second Coast Guard District, based in St. Louis, takes charge. In the Ohio River basin, the Coast Guard patrols from Owensboro, Kentucky. The Hudson River from New York to Watervliet is scouted by the Third Coast Guard District, based at Governors Island. North of Watervliet the river is under the jurisdiction of local sheriffs and police. The St. Johns River is patrolled by a Coast Guard station based at Mayport, Florida.

Charts and Publications

For charts and other up-to-date information on the river he wishes to cruise, the boatman can write to the following agencies.

> *For the Sacramento, San Joaquin and tributaries:*
> National Ocean Survey
> Distribution Division, C44
> 6501 Lafayette Avenue
> Riverdale, Maryland 20840
>
> *For the Colorado and its lakes:*
> U.S. Geological Survey
> Branch of Distribution, Central Region
> Box 25286, Federal Center
> Denver, Colorado 80225
>
> *For the Mississippi:*
> U.S. Army Engineer District St. Louis
> Office of Administrative Services
> 210 North 12th Street
> Room 942
> St. Louis, Missouri 63101
>
> *For the Ohio River basin:*
> U.S. Army Engineer Division
> Ohio River
> P.O. Box 1159
> Cincinnati, Ohio 45201
>
> *For the Hudson River and Lake Champlain:*
> National Ocean Survey
> Distribution Division, C44
> 6501 Lafayette Avenue
> Riverdale, Maryland 20840
>
> *For the St. Johns River:*
> National Ocean Survey
> Distribution Division, C44
> 6501 Lafayette Avenue
> Riverdale, Maryland 20840

The following publications give useful guidance on harbors, local facilities, fishing and the like.

> *Ohio River—Small Boat Harbors, Ramps, Landings.* Cincinnati: U.S. Army Engineer Division.
> *Quimby's Harbor Guide to the Entire Navigable Mississippi River.* Prairie du Chien, Wisconsin.
> Walters, Robert E., *Cruising the California Delta.* San Francisco: Miller Freeman Publications, Inc.
> *Waterway Guide, Northern Edition.* Annapolis, Maryland: Marine Annuals, Inc.
> *Waterway Guide, Southern Edition.* Annapolis, Maryland: Marine Annuals, Inc.

Getting ready to go fishing, a boatman lowers a small power launch from a 57-foot custom trawler lying just off Tinsley Island, where quiet Whiskey Slough runs off the San Joaquin River about 10 miles west of Stockton. Salmon, trout, steelhead, striped bass, catfish and crayfish are just a few of the species that abound in the delta waters.

Second-story porches hang over the sidewalks of the Sacramento River town of Locke, an old Chinese settlement. The town's clapboard living quarters and gambling dens —once the haunt of laborers who worked the levees—have become art and curio shops today. Visiting boatmen can tie up about a mile downriver at Walnut Grove, where merchants provide free docking alongside drugstores, grocery and hardware stores.

The California Delta

Though the California Delta lies in the embrace of Sacramento and Stockton, two busy deepwater ports, it nonetheless offers the pleasure boatman a remarkably tranquil and rural cruising ground. A snug little area no bigger than 24 by 48 miles, it is made up of scores of low islands and more than 1,000 miles of twisting green-brown rivers, sloughs, inlets and man-made cuts formed by the confluence of some half-dozen rivers, including the Sacramento and San Joaquin.

Whether the boatman comes into the delta from San Francisco Bay—in company with massive freighters and tankers—or launches a trailered craft from any of 50 or more public and private ramps in the delta's upper reaches, he is totally encompassed by a mariner's world. Virtually everyone here lives by water. Prestigious yacht-club anchorages give shelter to every kind of pleasure boat, from elaborate yawls to simple runabouts; many a private home has its own moorings—even the mailman from Stockton makes his rounds in an outboard-powered runabout. The region's rich agriculture is also a dividend of the liberally watered land. Behind the levees that rise to port and to starboard lie acres and acres of lettuce, asparagus, alfalfa, nuts, pears and grapes.

For the cruising boatman with no yacht-club affiliations there are dozens of public marinas; alternately, he can simply loop a line around a willow tree or drop anchor as he chooses. From nearby his mooring, he can fish in quiet seclusion practically all year round, or water-ski in summer on lanes that are set aside for the purpose—some of them six miles long. Or he can go ashore to wander among historical relics of the high-living age when stern-wheelers churned up from San Francisco with their cargo of gold-seekers, and dine in cosmopolitan restaurants redolent of the region's polyglot past.

The retired paddle-wheeler Delta King floats at a pier along a quiet stretch of the Sacramento River. In an era when paddle-wheelers were an essential means of transportation in this section of northern California, Delta King ran nightly between Sacramento and San Francisco, alternating with her sister ship, Delta Queen (page 60).

Less than a mile off the Deep Water Channel heading into Stockton, a row of boldly painted private boathouses stand reflected in the Calaveras River. In addition to housing their craft on their own property, delta boatmen can tie up at one of 7,500 berths that are maintained at the area's two dozen yacht clubs and more than 100 marinas.

LAKE POWELL

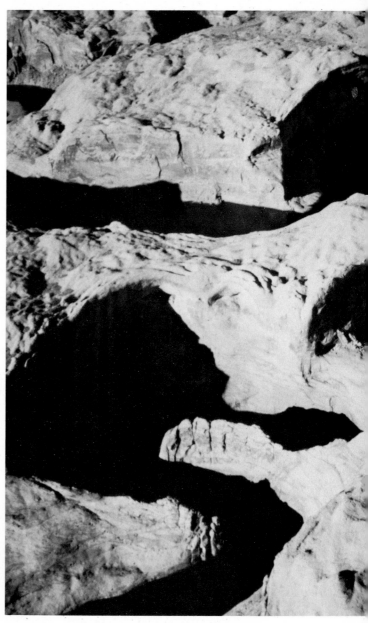

The serpentine walls of the Escalante River, an offshoot of the Colorado, dwarf a powerboat cutting a wispy wake at the base of 500-foot cliffs. Once an unnavigable stream, the Escalante was opened for boating as Lake Powell's waters rose. Near Willow Creek, a small stream that runs into the Escalante about seven miles from its mouth, the park service has restored a 700-year-old pueblo built on a ledge by the Anasazi Indians, who may be ancestors of the Hopi.

Rainbow Bridge arches over a finger of Lake Powell that has spilled into a natural redoubt called Forbidden Canyon. An awesome 278 feet in width, and soaring some 300 feet high, Rainbow is the largest natural bridge in the world. A Navajo legend says that a god, trapped here by a flood, prayed to a fellow spirit for help, and got it in the form of a rainbow, which turned to stone as he strode across it.

In one of the canyons off Lake Powell, a boy rows off in a dinghy to explore while his family remains aboard its cruiser to fish. More than 91 major canyons and hundreds of lesser ones lead off the lake, offering secluded anchorage for overnighting—for fishing in waters abundantly stocked with rainbow trout, bluegill, walleyed pike, kokanee salmon and largemouth bass reputed to be 10-pounders.

The Colorado

The mighty Colorado River is one of the unlikeliest cruising grounds anywhere. Winding between towering canyon walls that rise to a stony desert, its monstrous rapids have been impounded at scattered points to form four dazzling lakes, the largest and most inviting of which is Lake Powell. Beginning at Glen Canyon in northern Arizona, Lake Powell meanders northward for 186 miles to Hite, Utah. Rarely more than a mile wide, the lake sends out fingers of sapphire-blue water into hundreds of labyrinthine canyons, so that its total shoreline measures an astonishing 2,000 miles.

The sun shines virtually every day here, occasionally cooking the desert air to 100° between June and August. But from dawn till midmorning, and from 4 p.m. to about dusk, the temperature stays below 85° even in the summer. And nights are in the 60s. On summer afternoons occasional thunderstorms blow in suddenly from the west, and the winds that come with them, ricocheting off one canyon face after another, sometimes churn up six-foot waves. Otherwise, Lake Powell is as still as a puddle.

Because of the tricky winds and the narrow passages, Lake Powell is a place primarily for powerboats—and small dinghies for exploration in the shallower canyons. A boatman can trailer his craft to any of four marinas set at approximately 50-mile intervals on the lake's shore. Once launched, he is in a raw wilderness where an occasional wild burro brays in the distance and tiny canyon wrens trill nearby, their calls echoing in the resonant caverns. When the day's cruising is done, he can tether his craft to a boulder or beach it on a sandy shore, and explore the side canyons, with their fascinating rock forms, occasional Indian relics—and even dinosaur footprints etched into the sandstone 170 million years ago.

A quiet stretch of the upper Mississippi lies beneath the 300-foot bluffs of Palisades State Park at Savanna, Illinois. The park contains a dozen 2,000- to 6,000-year-old Indian burial mounds and is a haven for pileated woodpeckers and white-tailed deer. Its 10 miles of trails lead along cliffs strewn with rare flowers, including several species that survived the ice age, such as jeweled shooting stars and cliff goldenrod. At the foot of the bluffs, boatmen can moor at a dock owned by the State Department of Conservation.

The gleaming stainless-steel Gateway to the West soars 630 feet high over the St. Louis waterfront. Halfway between the Mississippi's head of commercial navigation and New Orleans, this booming city with its industrialized waterfront is, unfortunately, short on marinas. But a number of historic riverboats, moored at the city's national park and doing modern duty as restaurants, will allow a few visiting cruisers to tie up long enough for a meal. Local boatmen moor their craft at Alton, Illinois, 25 miles upstream.

On the lower Mississippi, a diesel-powered towboat dwarfs a sailing craft, whose skipper has unstepped his mast for passage under a nearby fixed bridge, one of eight on this stretch of river. Mississippi towboats push rather than pull their trains of barges, which sometimes total more than 1,000 feet in length; if the barges were trailed astern they might veer into a bank or shoal in the crosscurrents at the river's bends. Pleasure boats must give barges a wide berth and never cross directly in front; the tow's wake can swamp a small pleasure craft, and the bargeman needs up to a mile to halt his massive charge.

Stanton Hall, in Natchez, its stately columns and delicate grillwork asserting antebellum opulence, is the most imposing of some 30 Natchez mansions open to the public. The Greek Revival showplace was built in 1858 for cotton broker Frederick Stanton, who made his fortune after the introduction of steam-driven paddle-wheelers allowed merchants to ship goods upstream as well as down. Along with its ample opportunities for sightseeing, Natchez is one of the relatively few provisioning spots for cruisers on the lower river; there are no other ports for private boats for 65 miles in either direction.

The Mississippi

Any boatman setting forth to cruise the Mississippi may find himself a Lilliputian in giants' territory. The river's upper navigable reaches are dominated by long trains of 195-foot grain barges from Minneapolis and St. Paul. In the Gulf ports about 1,800 miles south, freighters bearing Russian, Japanese and other foreign flags put in to fetch the river's crops and the manufactures of their cities. Along the stretches between, the boatman is surrounded by a growing armada of other commercial vessels. Yet somehow the great river absorbs all this traffic and still leaves plenty of room for casual cruising.

To a boatman who travels its entire length, the Mississippi seems like two separate rivers, one flowing into the other. Along the upper 850 miles from Minneapolis and St. Paul to Cairo, Illinois, 26 locks and dams stem the current, creating a series of smooth, elongated lakes. For long stretches of the trip, the boatman slips past high bluffs and small islands, many of which the Fish and Wildlife Service maintains as wildlife sanctuaries. Marinas dot the wooded shoreline every 10 or 20 miles, so that launching and docking facilities are always close at hand.

Below Cairo the river swells to a mile or more in width. The locks and dams disappear, and 40-foot concrete levees wall the river—concealing broad cotton and rice fields, which stretch for miles beyond the riverbanks, and the lordly mansions that survive from antebellum times. There are few facilities for pleasure craft. But the bargemen are friendly, and will often shout a word of piloting advice, offer tips on weather and shoal conditions, and sometimes throw a line for tying up alongside a city levee.

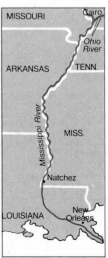

Cutting through the richly forested
Appalachian Mountains of Pennsylvania,
the Allegheny River broadens near the town
of Kittanning from a meandering stream into
a cruisable avenue. Here the river starts on
the final leg of its journey toward Pittsburgh,
where it empties into the Ohio.

Delta Queen—one of two American
passenger stern-wheelers still in active service
—steams down the Ohio from Cincinnati as
it heads toward New Orleans on the
Mississippi. Taking a leisurely seven and a
half days each way for the voyage, Delta
Queen provides a nostalgic excursion on
which vacationers can promenade the decks
or lounge in mahogany-paneled saloons
whose stained-glass windows are set in
copper. Plainer versions of such stern-
wheelers moved many settlers west in the
19th Century, when the Ohio served as a
major highway in the expansion of the nation.

Three cabin cruisers raft up on a dammed up section of the Cumberland—Lake Barkley, which, with Kentucky Lake, forms the Land Between the Lakes. Altogether the area offers 300 miles of shoreline, three large campgrounds and hundreds of solitary coves. The peninsula's 170,000 wilderness acres harbor wild turkey and buffalo—just as they did in pioneer days. The Tennessee Valley Authority, which maintains the area, runs a conservation center that offers visitors the opportunity to study natural history, fish for catfish and crappie, or hunt turkey, pheasant, duck and deer in season.

The Hunter Museum of Art, a renovated mansion built in Classic Revival style at the turn of the century, crowns a tree-fringed cliff overlooking the Tennessee River in Chattanooga. The visiting boatman can dock at nearby James Ross' Landing to visit the Hunter Museum, tour a host of Civil War sites, or take a ride on a Chattanooga choo-choo at the Tennessee Valley Railroad Museum.

The Ohio Basin

Four of the major watercourses of the Ohio River basin—the Allegheny, the Cumberland, the Tennessee and the lordly Ohio itself—stream through the smoke-belching heart of industrial America. Even so, the region's steel mills, coal mines, and chemical and hydroelectric plants cover only minuscule segments of the basin's 204,000 square miles. And despite 150 years of heavy use by industry, the rivers still flow by long stretches of unmarked forests and fields. Moreover, they provide the boatman with a voyage through country laden with American history.

Prehistoric Indians farmed along the Ohio and prerevolutionary trappers took beaver pelts from the Allegheny. Twice, George Washington floated down the Ohio—first as a young major surveying the region in 1753, and then as a private citizen seeking land to develop in 1770. And Union General Ulysses S. Grant, in his first important Civil War victories, took Fort Henry on the Tennessee River and Fort Donelson on the Cumberland.

For amateur botanists, the Tennessee may well be the most intriguing of these rivers. Near Chattanooga it cuts through a gorge that Tennesseans like to call the Grand Canyon of the South. Some 150 varieties of trees grow there, and in fall create a panoply of color that may be unmatched anywhere else in the United States. Chattanooga boat clubs celebrate this spectacle with a cruise through the gorge in late October every year, and all comers are welcome.

In any month from June to October, the basin's rivers are likely to provide convivial cruising. Virtually every town along the way has mooring docks and launching ramps, from which more than 100,000 weekend sailors and campers regularly embark. And for any boatman with a yen for privacy, there are plenty of coves and tributaries where he can drop a fish line, water-ski or just laze in solitude in the sun.

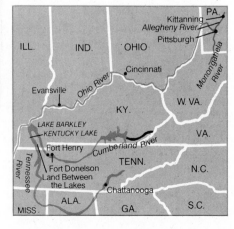

The Hudson

Not far north of Manhattan, a boatman heading upstream along the Hudson River cruises past one of the greenest and most gracefully contoured shorelines on the Atlantic seaboard. For a few miles he glides beneath the cliffs of New Jersey's Palisades, then between high wooded escarpments that inspired the romantic canvases of America's 19th Century landscape artists of the so-called Hudson River School. In the hills are the estates—some visible from the water—of such past notables as Washington Irving, Frederick W. Vanderbilt and Franklin D. Roosevelt.

Farther upstream, the boatman moves through an ever-changing mix of fresh river water and tidal salt water from the Atlantic. The river bed, dug by a powerful ancestral stream, extends 150 miles into the ocean, cutting a broad scoop into the continental shelf. The incoming tide funnels daily into this channel and sweeps upstream as far as Troy. The tidewater alleviates industrial and human waste, and brings in a rich array of salt-water fish.

The boatman can work the tide to his own advantage in either direction—timing a day's run to coincide with ebb or flow, and using the layover time for visits ashore. Almost every village along the way has a marina or yacht club.

Though Troy is the head of commercial salt-water navigation, a cruising boatman can continue on. He can cut west along the 350-mile New York State Barge Canal, by the rolling country of the Mohawk Valley. Or he can go north, past the 10 toll-free locks of the Champlain Canal, past herds of dairy cattle into the farmlands beyond. Then, 186 nautical miles above New York City, he slips onto Lake Champlain, which leads to Canada's Richelieu River and eventually the St. Lawrence.

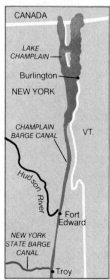

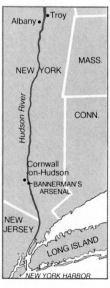

A yawl heading north along the lower Hudson River sails beneath the 110-story towers of the World Trade Center at Manhattan's tip. Less than a mile east, old sailing ships and steam vessels lie permanently moored at the South Street Seaport Museum on a partly restored 19th Century waterfront. Five miles north, the 79th Street Boat Basin has 145 slips for pleasure craft, only 10 of them for transients. Manhattan has few other attractions for the cruising sailor—although in summer hundreds of pleasure boats brave the three-knot currents and urban debris to make the 35-mile circuit of New York's shoreline.

A mansion called Bannerman's Arsenal overlooks the Hudson River near Cornwall, some 50 miles north of New York City. The imposing building was erected in 1908 by Francis Bannerman, a wealthy munitions dealer, who hoped to imbue the Hudson with a feudal grandeur reminiscent of medieval Scotland. The interior, together with Bannerman's prize collection of antique weaponry, burned in 1971, but the turreted façade still frowns out at the river channel.

Near Burlington, Vermont, some 70 miles north of the barge canal leading in from the Hudson, Lake Champlain gleams in the sun setting over the distant Adirondacks. Winds sweep north and south on the 125-mile-long lake, sometimes churning its clear blue water into nasty whitecaps. But the lake's shore provides many coves for anchorage on both the New York and Vermont sides, along with a bumper crop of historic ports of call. Best known are Fort Ticonderoga, a British garrison that fell to colonial troops in 1775, and Valcour Island, where Benedict Arnold assembled the infant U.S. fleet in 1776.

The St. Johns

Florida's north-flowing St. Johns River is so rich with fish that a boatman cruising on it can hardly fail to haul in a scrappy—and eminently edible—catch. Some 118 species flourish here in huge numbers, among them crappie, pickerel, shad, catfish and so many bass that no one will ever come close to catching them all.

A cruising boatman can reach this fisherman's haven by heading west from the Atlantic across the Intracoastal Waterway at Mayport, which bills itself as the country's oldest fishing village (a band of Huguenots settled near here in 1564). In the next 12 miles, pleasure boats share the channel with freighters heading into Jacksonville. Then the river turns south—into a world of magnolia-filled lawns, citrus groves and cattle ranches. About 50 miles south of Jacksonville, the cruiser reaches Palatka, an old Indian river ford. And here the very best of St. Johns cruising begins.

For another 150 miles, past the Cross Florida Barge Canal and as far as Sanford (once a fashionable playground for *fin de siècle* Astors and Vanderbilts), the boatman floats through a serene and indolent jungle. Here turtles doze in the sun, and bald eagles, whippoorwills, ospreys and quail call from moss-hung cypress, bay trees, live oak and palmetto that shade the riverbanks. If he looks hard, the boatman will discover here and there, in a bend in the river, an unpretentious dock where he can fill up on gas and bait, and maybe get a good meal. A few of the back-country restaurants will even cook the fisherman's own catch—in deep fat, rolled in flour and cornmeal, the way a proper southern fish is supposed to be cooked.

Beyond a floating island of water hyacinth—a prolific weed that so clogs propellers and blocks channels in Florida waters that the Corps of Engineers must constantly spray to control it—two anglers laze in the mirror-smooth Wekiva River, a shallow backwater of the St. Johns. Among the prime fishing waters along the St. Johns, the Wekiva is particularly noted for its bass, which tend to congregate close to the protection that is offered by such hyacinth islands. The shaded shoreline, thick with live oak and cypress trees overhung with Spanish moss, is a refuge for bear, raccoon, egret and limpkin.

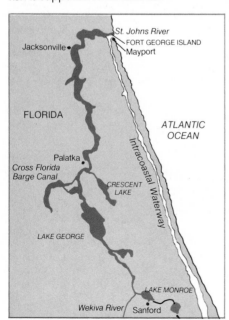

Perched on a pile of bleached fallen logs that blend with its sandy brown fur, a river otter thrusts up its snout and sniffs the air. Playful and inquisitive, it may surprise a fisherman in the backwaters of the St. Johns by popping up beside his skiff; the quick little creature, which lives in dens with underwater entrances, will just as suddenly disappear to dive for the fish and crustaceans on which it feeds.

A lightning-struck live oak tree spreads its branches out over the east shore of Lake George. Eleven miles long and five to seven miles wide, the lake is the largest of a series of broad lagoons along the course of the St. Johns River. Its sandy shores are unusually barren in this otherwise jungled region. The lake's west shore (background) is shoal, but a 12-foot channel in the center connects with the St. Johns at both ends.

Kingsley Plantation, once the home of a slave-trading magnate and now a museum, stands behind a row of palms on Fort George Island. The island has no docks for visiting craft, but can be reached by a 15-minute ferry ride from Mayport, first port of call for boatmen cruising upstream into the St. Johns.

4 Some first loves will suffice for a lifetime, and so it has been for me in my continuing romance with the Great Lakes. I started cruising them before World War II, as a 16-year-old sea scout whose home port was landbound River Forest, Illinois, 10 miles from Chicago. The ship, or troop, I belonged to owned a 50-foot Navy lifeboat converted to sail. On long summer weekends we would set out from Chicago across Lake Michigan to. the eastern shore. We would catch the prevailing southwest wind and sail all Friday night, escaping the awful heat that surrounds Chicago in July and August. Saturday morning we would be in St. Joseph, Michigan. From there we would coast

THE GREAT LAKES SEAWAY

down to Michigan City following the sandy pine-backed shore, then make an easy run home. En route, we might anchor offshore for a cooling swim in the clear lake water. But what we boys liked best was the chance to visit the amusement park on the beach at St. Joe.

Amusement parks now stand low on my list of cruising priorities, and it is other pleasures that draw me out onto the infinitely varied seaway we call the Great Lakes: the wild, waterworn caves of Lake Superior's Apostle Islands, or the solitude of Superior's northern coast, with its pine-shrouded headlands and its beaver, bear and moose. In Huron's North Channel I sometimes go ashore before breakfast to explore an island that I have all to myself, and perhaps pick a hatful of blueberries for pancakes. Or I may push on to Lake Ontario, to bask as a guest in the squirely pomp of the Royal Canadian Yacht Club in Toronto, which demands coat and tie at dinner, and to take a ride in the R.C.Y.C.'s 71-foot power launch, built in 1912 and manned by a crew decked out in starched shirts and brass buttons. Perhaps what intrigues me most about cruising the lakes is the distance between those starched shirts and the blueberry picking. I like variety, and in 37 years of traveling all five of the lakes through most kinds of weather aboard everything from a 19-foot sloop to a 60-foot converted Gulf Coast shrimp boat, I have never been bored. In fact, the lakes have kept me so fascinated that I have never really gone beyond them, never, in fact, handled a boat in an ocean sea.

My salt-water friends ask me how the lakes differ from ocean cruising. I tell them that I prefer the lakes, first, for their fresh water, which makes life afloat so much easier. Metal fittings last far longer in fresh water—and decks and brightwork do not forever need swabbing down. Swimming leaves you feeling fresh and clean. And there are still parts of Lake Superior and up north in Lake Huron where you can dip your hand in and drink.

I also like the challenges that fresh water makes on seamanship. There is always a lee shore to stay clear of and, away from the shipping lanes, a few uncharted rocks and shoals to keep a navigator on his toes. Storms come up —and can change course—with a suddenness of which salt-water skippers can barely conceive. In a matter of minutes, they churn up a fury of short, steep waves, and they have littered the lakes with wrecks. I was aboard a 55-foot ketch in June of 1946 when a fierce line squall hit us off Menominee in Green Bay, on Lake Michigan. We quickly struck all sails and rode out the storm under bare poles, tearing along at nine knots with our rail two feet under. But just a few miles to the south, the same 80-mile-an-hour winds and terrifying seas blasted a 35-foot sloop, sinking her with all hands save one—a lone girl who somehow survived the night in the chilly water.

For me the focus of the lakes, the pinwheel around which the rest turns, is the exuberant yachting center of Mackinac Island. Just three miles long, the island rises like the back of a turtle (Mackinac is derived from the Indian word meaning great turtle) in the middle of the Straits of Mackinac, where Lakes

Sculptured rock forms jut out from Devil's Island in Lake Superior's Apostle group, where the pounding of storms has gouged caves, tunnels and overhangs in the soft sandstone.

A native of Chicago, Art Hutchison has sailed the Great Lakes for more than 37 years. During that time he has competed in 15 Chicago-to-Mackinac races, has been editor for 25 years of the Great Lakes Cruising Club's Port Pilot and Log Book, and has served a two-year term as the club's commodore.

Michigan and Huron meet; and it is a haven for both cruising and racing men. Every July, annual races from Port Huron and Chicago finish here. The racing crews come heaving in after a grueling three-day grind, break out grog and guitars, and may wind up the celebration with dinner at the splendid old Grand Hotel (right).

The Grand Hotel is a thriving relic from the gracious 1880s, when plush steamers brought well-to-do families from Detroit, Saginaw, Chicago, Milwaukee and Green Bay to Mackinac Island for leisurely summer-long vacations. In fact, the whole island is redolent with history. Whenever I put in at the Mackinac yacht basin, and after taking a carriage up to the hotel golf club for a martini and a bowl of superb onion soup, I make it a point to visit various monuments of the island's past. John Jacob Astor's first fur-trading post, which Astor built in 1809 to deal in the beaver pelts that made his fortune, still stands right in town. On a hill overlooking the town is a British fort, now a museum, built in 1781 to control the fur trade through the straits.

Only a few mementos remain from the island's earliest white visitors: French explorers, missionaries and fur traders who arrived in their long canoes and paused here on their way west—and then put in again, if they were lucky, on their way back. One vessel that did not get back was the 60-foot two-masted Griffin, built in 1679 by the French explorer La Salle for the fur trade. The Griffin was the first sailing ship to navigate the lakes above Niagara Falls, and on her maiden voyage she headed west through the Straits of Mackinac, picked up furs in Green Bay—and then disappeared forever. It is standard sport on the lakes these days to hunt for her wreck.

For me, Mackinac Island makes a perfect base for exploring deeper into the lakes. From there I sometimes head north through the Soo Canal to adventure in wild and moody Lake Superior—being sure all hands have brought their long underwear and the cabin has a heater against the chilly summer nights. The Canadian fishing port of Mamainse Harbour on the eastern shore is my special choice for a first night's stop—and a good place to purchase fresh lake trout. Or sometimes I head back into Lake Michigan, steering southwest toward the shelter of Green Bay, under the towering limestone bluffs of Door County—where I remember one long midspring night, from my early sailing days, when breezes carried the scent of pine across the water and into my cabin. I remember, too, the tales of some of the area's saltier characters. My favorite is one Captain Dan Seavey, who had a reputation for sailing off with anything not nailed down, boats included, and selling it wherever he could around the lake. Eventually the village of Garden passed a resolution forbidding Seavey to put a mooring line on any of its docks. He came ashore anyway, simply by falling back on his anchor line until he was close enough to jump the distance to the dock.

My favorite course, however, is east across the top of Huron into the North Channel, and then into Georgian Bay with its 30,000 islands. (This part of the lakes, incidentally, is also accessible by road through Canada, and is so sheltered that I recommend it for trailered outboards.) The first Canadian island on the route is Cockburn (pronounced "Coburn"), with its quaint little port of Tolsmaville. Each night the lights here all go out at once—when the mayor turns off the generator on his way to bed. Only 25 years ago, Cockburn was a busy port that, like many up this way, made a living on fishing and lumber. Now many of the anchorages lie near abandoned sawmills; more than once I have dragged a Danforth across bottoms 10 feet thick in soggy sawdust.

For all their air of rustic sleepiness, many of the towns in the northern area of the Great Lakes periodically come back to life—thanks to a new wave of voyageurs. These new explorers sail mostly fiberglass hulls, and their purpose is to relax and have fun. I am pleased to count myself among them. And still I feel no need to go down to the salt sea. There is enough cruising for one lifetime to be done right here.

by Art Hutchison

An old opera wagon rolls past the elegant front of Mackinac Island's
Grand Hotel, which boasts the world's longest porch—880 feet of
it—overlooking the Straits of Mackinac and the five-mile span of the
Mackinac Bridge. Perhaps the most popular stopover for pleasure-
boaters cruising from Lake Michigan to Huron's North Channel, the
island permits transport only by horse and buggy or bicycle.

Giant Steps for Sailors

Sprawled mid-continent between a province of Canada and eight American states, covering 95,000 square miles and washing some 8,300 miles of shoreline, the five Great Lakes constitute the largest freshwater cruising ground in the world.

Beginning with Lake Superior, 600 feet above sea level, the glacier-carved basins drop eastward in a series of connecting stairs. The first step comes at the St. Marys River, where the waters surge down to Lake Huron, lying on the same level as Lake Michigan and connected to it by the Straits of Mackinac. They descend from eastern Huron through the St. Clair and Detroit rivers into Lake Erie, and then plunge headlong over Niagara Falls before flowing into Lake Ontario. At Ontario's northeastern end they squeeze into the shoal-strewn St. Lawrence on their way to the Atlantic.

For all these natural obstructions, boatmen can navigate the Great Lakes from end to end—thanks to some strategically placed canals. For example, at Sault Ste. Marie the Soo locks can lift boats from Lake Huron up to Lake Superior for voyages into wilderness spots such as Isle Royale *(pages 74-75)*. The Straits of Mackinac require no locks; they are a natural gateway for Chicago-based yachtsmen seeking the cool seclusion of Huron's North Channel and Georgian Bay.

A Buffalo boatman must use the eight-lock Welland Canal as a down escalator to bypass Niagara Falls and reach Ontario; or he can turn northeast up the Niagara River to Tonawanda and take the historic Erie Canal leading to the Hudson River. Most picturesque of all these man-made passages is the 240-mile-long Trent-Severn Waterway, linking Huron to Lake Ontario—and to the Thousand Islands at the headwaters of the St. Lawrence River.

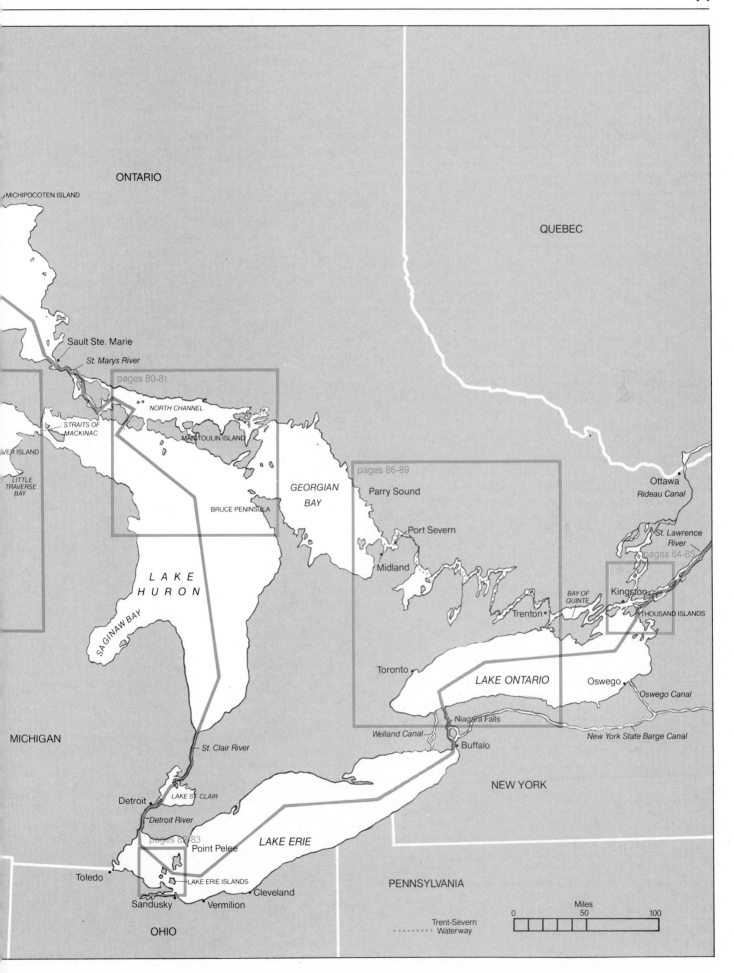

ONTARIO

MICHIPOCOTEN ISLAND

QUEBEC

Sault Ste. Marie

St. Marys River

pages 80-81

NORTH CHANNEL

STRAITS OF
MACKINAC

MANITOULIN ISLAND

...VER ISLAND

*LITTLE
TRAVERSE
BAY*

BRUCE PENINSULA

*GEORGIAN
BAY*

pages 86-89

Parry Sound

Port Severn

Midland

Ottawa

Rideau Canal

*St. Lawrence
River*

pages 84-85

*L A K E
H U R O N*

SAGINAW BAY

BAY OF
QUINTE

Kingston

THOUSAND ISLANDS

Trenton

Toronto

LAKE ONTARIO

Oswego

Oswego Canal

MICHIGAN

St. Clair River

LAKE ST. CLAIR

Detroit

Detroit River

pages 82-83

Point Pelee

LAKE ERIE

Niagara Falls

Welland Canal

Buffalo

NEW YORK

New York State Barge Canal

Toledo

LAKE ERIE ISLANDS

Cleveland

Sandusky

Vermilion

PENNSYLVANIA

OHIO

Miles

0   50   100

········· Trent-Severn
         Waterway

Winds and Weather

Though large areas of the Great Lakes freeze over with impassable ice during winter, they generally are open to commercial navigation from May through November. But for cruising, the comfortable season normally extends only from late June into September, with July and August the prime months.

Prevailing winds are southwesterly at 15 to 30 knots, with some notable exceptions. Lake Superior, with an enormous volume of very cold water (32° to 54°) surrounded by warmer land in summer, generates a high-pressure system with onshore breezes that blow in a clockwise direction. In Lake Huron's North Channel, the winds are generally either westerly or easterly.

Sudden and devastating thunderstorms, which can hit anywhere in the lakes, constitute the region's greatest boating hazard. Winds of 87 knots have been registered in Lake Erie in July. These storms signal their approach by advancing thunderheads or squall lines, and in shallow areas can kick up eight-foot seas in less than an hour. Wind storms of longer duration can also build high seas on the lakes; 20-foot waves are not unknown on Superior. Mariners should keep tuned to the weather forecast, and be ready to run for shelter if necessary.

Fog poses another hazard for Great Lakes sailors. It is most severe on Lake Superior and in the Straits of Mackinac from April through June, but summer fogs may occur in land-enclosed areas such as the Soo locks and around Lake Huron's islands.

Tides and Currents

Spring snowmelt makes water levels in the Great Lakes slightly higher in spring and summer than they are later in the year, but the overall change is no more than about three feet. A month-by-month tabulation can be found in the *Great Lakes Pilot.*

More substantial, though temporary, fluctuations are caused by strong winds blowing for extended periods, or by a combination of winds and rapid changes in barometric pressure. These phenomena can raise the water level on a lee shore by as much as seven or eight feet, particularly in shallow, confined areas such as Green Bay and the eastern and western shores of Lake Erie. Then, when the winds die, the accumulated water sweeps back across the lake in a powerful wave, or seiche. In open water, seiches are usually harmless, but they can hit the opposite lake front with destructive force.

Currents are not pronounced, except in narrow channels and waterways. At Little Current, on the North Channel, water can flow at 3.5 knots in either direction, and eight-knot currents are common along certain stretches of the upper Niagara River. Boatmen should also anticipate strong and sometimes erratic currents at the downstream end of a lock.

Pilotage

With an annual traffic of some 7,000 freighters and ore boats, the Great Lakes contain some of the most heavily traveled shipping lanes in the world. These lanes are marked with distinctive dashed lines on the chart, and pleasure craft should avoid them. Boatmen should note that the lakes have their own right-of-way rules, which employ distinctive horn signals and give precedence to vessels bound downstream in channels with currents.

Most channels and harbors in the Great Lakes are well marked with navigational aids. The principal exceptions are Huron's North Channel and Georgian Bay, whose shallow waters are so packed with rocks that many are unmarked and uncharted. Floating debris is a problem in Lake Superior, where logs that have drifted loose from pulpwood floats become a menace.

Before cruising any of the waterways on the lakes, the skipper should check allowances for draft and overhead clearances. To complete passage on the Trent-Severn, for instance, draft cannot exceed four feet on the Big Chute marine railway.

Mast-height limitations are equally critical. Boats higher than 22 feet on the Trent-Severn or 20 feet on the New York State Barge Canal cannot traverse portions of the system. In dense island areas such as Georgian Bay, watch for overhead electric lines, whose heights often differ from those listed.

Boats and Special Equipment

Powerboats and sailing craft of virtually every size and description can cruise comfortably on the lakes—depending on the particular area. Thus, full-keel sailboats and deep-draft power vessels are the most suitable craft for the rugged and relatively isolated upper reaches of Lake Superior—and because of the distance between ports, powerboats should have a fuel capacity for passages of up to 125 miles. Smaller, lighter-displacement powerboats, on the other hand, are excellent for the island areas of northeastern Lake Huron and in the protected waterways.

A good compass is essential for Great Lakes cruising. Sailors should take note, however, that large magnetic variations, probably caused by iron-ore deposits, occur along the north shore of Lake Superior, the north end of the North Channel near Magnetic Reefs, and at Kingston Harbor on Lake Ontario. In these waters, be sure to check bearings against charted landmarks.

All boats should carry an AM-FM transistor radio for local weather reports, or better yet a VHF ship-to-shore set. The U.S. National Weather Service broadcasts continuous forecasts on FM at 162.55 and 162.40 mHz. A dependable radio direction finder will aid piloting when visibility is poor, and prudent boatmen will always hoist a radar reflector near shipping lanes.

The rocky bottoms of Lake Superior, Georgian Bay and the North Channel call for a good holding anchor, such as a yachtsman. Elsewhere, a Danforth or plow will usually provide security. But two anchors are always the best protection in difficult situations. For rocky areas, a spare propeller and shaft are advisable. And anyone passing through locks will need stout fender boards and heavy mooring lines—at least one 75-foot line for the Soo locks, and two 100-foot lines for the Welland Canal.

Bring warm clothing, foul-weather gear and sea boots. And, for cruising icy waters, carry insulated flotation jackets.

Wildlife

Enormous stretches of protected wilderness line the Great Lakes shore fronts, all rich in wildlife. The U.S. side contains one national park, four national lakeshore areas and more than 50 state parks. On the Canadian side, sailors can visit four national and 32 provincial parks. Many of these lie within the flyways of migratory birds, and in spring and fall the skies over Lakes Huron, Erie and Ontario teem with ducks, whistler swans and Canada geese. And all along the lakes, even outside park boundaries, boatmen will find a plenitude of animal life—from black bear and moose in the pine forests of Lake Superior to the white-tailed deer that range south from Georgian Bay to Lake Ontario.

Sports

Bass, northern pike, perch, muskellunge, lake trout, walleye and pickerel abound in the Great Lakes, the Thousand Islands and the Canadian canals. Most U.S. states and the province of Ontario sell licenses on a limited-use or an annual basis.

For swimming and water-skiing, Lake Erie is the shallowest and warmest; its waters reach 75° in late summer and fall. Warm pockets can be found on all the lakes, and along the waterways in sun-warmed bays and inlets. Most areas of Lake Superior are too cold for more than a quick dip.

Scuba diving is popular in areas like Gills Rock at the end of the Door Peninsula, off Tobermory on the Bruce Peninsula, and the Lake Erie islands near scores of wrecked ships.

Regional Boating Regulations

All craft entering Canadian waters must be properly licensed at their place of origin and must secure a cruising permit from Canadian customs. A list of entry ports can be obtained from the customs office at the Canadian Consul General in New York. Upon departure, the boatman must surrender the permit; but he need not check in with U.S. customs unless carrying declarable merchandise. As a courtesy, a Canadian ensign should be flown while in Canadian territory.

Canadian national parks require a small docking fee, and Canadian waterways with locking systems charge for a daily, short-term or seasonal permit. On the Welland Canal there is a charge for each lock, and because of the locks' enormous size, boats must meet minimum requirements of 20 feet in length and a ton in weight. In addition, the Canadian government requires boats on the Welland to carry the *Seaway Handbook* and Canadian chart 2042; they must also pick up the latest marine notices at either end of the canal. Similarly, boats traveling the Trent-Severn and Rideau must carry the *Canal Regulations*.

Major Provisioning Ports

As the boatman proceeds from Lake Superior into the other lakes, the number of provisioning ports increases. Here are some of the principal ones, listed by lake, from Superior to Ontario. They all offer sheltered marinas, fuel pumps, marine and food stores, repair yards and hospital facilities.

Bayfield: On the Wisconsin shore of Lake Superior; a charming fishing village, and the main departure point for cruising the Apostle Islands.

Sault Ste. Marie: The largest city on the eastern end of Lake Superior, and a port of entry into Canada; the last spot for at least 100 miles to obtain charts and other special nautical supplies.

Sturgeon Bay: A bustling town that offers the most complete boating facilities on Lake Michigan's Door Peninsula.

Little Current: A favorite launching site in Ontario for cruises into Lake Huron's North Channel and the northern end of Georgian Bay.

Midland: In Ontario at the southeast corner of Georgian Bay; a perfect take-off point for cruising the bay's islands or the Trent-Severn.

Kingston: The largest Canadian port on eastern Lake Ontario; ideally situated for visiting the Thousand Islands or taking a trip up the Rideau Canal.

Coast Guard Stations

The Cleveland-based Ninth Coast Guard District maintains 41 regular stations and six auxiliary stations around the lakes. A continuous radio watch is maintained on distress frequencies 2182 kHz and 156.80 mHz by many U.S. Coast Guard stations and a number of radio-equipped boats. All five Canadian Coast Guard stations and eight Canadian Coast Guard radio stations also monitor these frequencies on a 24-hour basis.

Charts and Publications

The Great Lakes are covered by U.S. National Ocean Survey charts 14500-14976, by Canadian Hydrographic Service charts 2000-2400, and by the Great Lakes light lists of the U.S. and Canada, Great Lakes Rules of the Road and Great Lakes *Pilots* of both countries (*Canadian Pilot*, Vol. I, contains the canal systems and waters west to Lake St. Clair; Vol. II, the St. Clair River to Lake Superior). For applicable charts, see *U.S. Nautical Chart Catalog 4* and *Canadian Nautical Charts, Bulletin 1*. References from both countries should be used. All charts are updated regularly by Canadian and U.S. Ninth District Coast Guard's *Notices to Mariners*. The Great Lakes are covered by U.S. Marine Weather Service Charts MSC-11 and MSC-12; and Canada's Department of Indian and Northern Affairs publishes canal regulations. The most recent editions of these can be obtained by writing to the appropriate government agencies, with the Superintendent of Documents supplying the U.S. light list, and the Coast Guard in Washington, D.C., the Rules of the Road.

National Ocean Survey
Distribution Division, C44
6501 Lafayette Avenue
Riverdale, Maryland 20840

Superintendent of Documents
U.S. Government Printing Office
Washington, D.C. 20402

Commandant (G-BA-2)
Boating Information Branch
U.S. Coast Guard
Washington, D.C. 20590

U.S. Coast Guard, Ninth District
1240 East Ninth Street
Cleveland, Ohio 44199

Hydrographic Chart Distribution Office
Department of the Environment
1675 Russell Road
Ottawa, Ontario, Canada, K1A0E6

Department of Indian and Northern Affairs
Canal Division
365 Laurier Street
Ottawa, Ontario, Canada, K1A0H4

One of the most valuable cruising guides to the lakes is the *Port Pilot and Log Book*, published by the Chicago-based Great Lakes Cruising Club and available to members. Other helpful publications are:

Cruising Mid-America, Vol. II. Ann Arbor, Michigan: Boating Publications, Inc.

Waterway Guide, Northern Edition. Annapolis, Maryland: Marine Annuals, Inc.

Yachtsman's Guide to the Great Lakes. Grand Rapids, Michigan: Seaport Publishing Co.

Lake Superior

Nowhere in America will a cruising boat-man find such broad expanses of un-touched wilderness as along the north shore of Lake Superior. The lake is Hia-watha's "shining Big-Sea Water," and its upper reaches still exist much as the In-dians knew them. The evergreen forest along the Canadian side is alive with bear, moose, beaver and grouse. Scores of nat-ural harbors indent the shore.

But this is no place for the dilettante sailor or for boats under 20 feet. The wa-ter here is indeed big, often rough, beset by sudden fogs and storms, and it is al-ways cold, averaging a numbing 32° to 40° even on summer days. Along some stretches, more than 100 miles may sep-arate fuel-and-food facilities. For exam-ple, Michipicoten Island lies two or three days' sail north from the Soo locks. And though it offers a superb, two-mile-long harbor, the only provisions a visitor will find are six- to eight-pound trout—which he must catch himself.

The American shore to the south is more populous and industrial. Even so, a boatman is never far from wilderness. A 55-mile run from the ore docks and freighter terminals of Duluth leads to the nearest of the Apostle Islands (page 66), where the tide of civilization has been re-versed: after years of occupation by com-mercial fishermen, stone quarriers and lumberjacks, the Apostles are now a wild-life sanctuary. Elsewhere, Indian reserva-tions, abandoned copper mines, a historic wooden fort and 200-foot-high sandstone bluffs dot the lake front.

A passage through the Keweenaw Pen-insula via the Keweenaw Waterway leads a westward-traveling boatman toward the Isle Royale archipelago (map, below), the most interesting wilderness area of all. Here a U.S. national park shelters Canada geese, rare pileated woodpeckers, red fox, beaver and a herd of 1,000 moose.

This lone cow moose cooling herself in an Isle Royale stream is a descendant of a small herd that crossed over the ice from Canada in a bitter winter around 1910. The herd began to outgrow its food supply, until another immigrant, the eastern timber wolf, crossed the ice in 1948 and started keeping the moose in check.

ISLE ROYALE

A massive basalt headland guards the shoal-ridden entrance to Rock Harbor on Isle Royale, dominant island of the group bearing its name. The largest land mass in Superior, this 45-mile-long refuge has no roads or wheeled vehicles to disturb its wildlife. However, docking facilities, fuel, food and potable water are available at Rock Harbor Marina and in Washington Harbor on the island's southwestern tip.

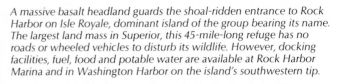

The flashing beacon on tiny Rock of Ages Island glimmers through one of Superior's frequent fogs, warning boats of the reefs and shoals lying around the southwestern end of Isle Royale. Commissioned in 1908, the 117-foot-high light operates from April through January, closing down when all local yachting and even commercial shipping stops as the winter ice closes in.

More than 170 miles of foot trails—planked in swampy areas—crisscross the main island, leading to trout-filled streams and to lakelets jumping with perch and walleye. Hikers and fishermen are cautioned that no pets are permitted ashore or even aboard visiting boats—a regulation designed to protect native wildlife against possible infection with distemper, fleas, dysentery or rabies.

The verdant resort village of Ephraim on Door Peninsula retains a slow-paced 19th Century charm, even when summer swells the population from 250 to 2,500—and more during regatta week in August. Ephraim's harbor offers ample swing room for more than 70 boats; the bottom is gravel and ranges from four to 10 feet deep. Part of the municipal pier provides several transient berths for cruising craft of up to 50 feet.

The fish boil—Door Peninsula's contribution to the culinary world—serves as the gastronomic mainstay of lakeshore picnics, church socials and open-air restaurants during the sailing season. The dish consists of boiled whitefish or trout with potatoes and onions, served with butter. A regional specialty for over 100 years, the fish boil probably originated with hungry lumberjacks in need of robust, easily concocted fare.

Lake Michigan

The shores of Lake Michigan, like those of Huron to the east, present two distinctly contrasting landscapes for cruising. The lake's western, or Wisconsin, shoreline is rocky and rugged; it is almost bare of docks or services for pleasure craft—until the boatman arrives at the resort area of Door Peninsula (map, below).

Jabbing into Lake Michigan to form Green Bay, this beguiling region of tidy clapboard villages, pine woods and cherry orchards derives its name from early French explorers, who called the passage at its northern tip Porte des Morts (the Door of the Dead)—and with good reason. Here, violent storms may stir up erratic and hazardous currents among the passageway's shoals and reefs. Today, yachtsmen heading into the protected harbors of Green Bay are able to avoid this northern portal altogether by passing through the toll-free canal at Sturgeon Bay, where several privately owned marinas offer fuel and repairs.

The lake's eastern shore is sandy and benign. The state of Michigan has created small noncommercial harbors every 30 miles or so along the shore by dredging out river mouths or remodeling disused lumber and trading ports.

A boatman idling northward from Chicago passes an ever-changing panorama of resorts, beaches, river inlets and forest reserves that lead up to a spectacular slice of wilderness: Sleeping Bear Dunes (overleaf), where the wind has exposed the bleached bones of trees after centuries of interment under sand. He can anchor and swim at nearby Beaver Island, site of a 19th Century Mormon settlement founded by James Strang—who reigned as king until rebellious subjects murdered him. Or he may head into Little Traverse Bay (overleaf) for a taste of elegant living in an area renowned for its posh yacht clubs and restaurants.

Yachtsmen visiting the small resort town of Egg Harbor on Green Bay can take a sightseeing junket along the wooded shoreline in this replica of a 19th Century stagecoach, reminiscent of early local transport. Egg Harbor is often the first stop after Sturgeon Bay for northbound pleasure craft, which must anchor in 34-foot-deep rock-bottomed waters or tie up at a dock accommodating about 30 boats.

A salvaged cargo ship, Alvin Clark, squats firmly in the mud at Menominee, Michigan, a short sail across Green Bay from Door Peninsula. Built in 1846, the 220-ton brigantine sank in a storm in 1864 and was raised from the silt by local divers in 1969. Typical of 19th Century freighters on the Great Lakes, this beamy 113-footer carried a centerboard that could be retracted for entering shallow harbors to pick up cargoes of grain, coal, lumber and salt.

LAKE MICHIGAN: LITTLE TRAVERSE BAY

Luxurious condominium colonies and an adjacent marina grace the shore front of Harbor Springs on Little Traverse Bay, a favorite summering spot for prosperous Midwesterners. On summer weekends, up to 500 boats may anchor in its mile-wide harbor. At the first-rate public dock, water depth is 20 feet, and art galleries, boutiques —and tennis courts with night lighting—are just a short stroll away.

A sprightly gaff-rigged cutter glides to windward out of Harbor Springs, its topsail bagged at the masthead where it can be broken out easily. Shallow of draft and broad of beam, the 42-footer is a slightly modernized cruising version of the speedy but stable Lake Michigan fishing smacks common in the early part of the century.

A classic Great Lakes racing sloop, this 32-foot Northern Michigan rocks gently at its mooring only yards away from the green lawns of Harbor Point, near Harbor Springs. Designed in 1934, the Northern Michigans enjoyed years of popularity throughout Traverse Bay communities. The survivors of the class, all based in Harbor Springs, still compete on weekends in July and August.

On calm days cruising boatmen can anchor off Sleeping Bear Dunes National Lakeshore, a long day's sail southwest of Little Traverse Bay, and row in for a picnic on the beach. Or they can put in at nearby Glen Haven and charter a dune buggy for an excursion into the dunes themselves. These towering sand hills—some over 400 feet high—are constantly, if imperceptibly, growing: waves gouge into submerged sand and drive it ashore, and storms fling it up the dune walls.

Lake Huron

Even Lake Huron's most ardent admirers concede that the busy west-lake commercial routes from Port Huron to the Straits of Mackinac hold little joy for cruising yachtsmen. But along the northeastern shores of the lake, separated from its main body by Manitoulin Island and the Bruce Peninsula, lie two of the most bewitching of all inland cruising grounds: the North Channel and Georgian Bay, together encompassing an area of about 6,000 square miles. Wild, and to a large extent uncharted, these waters are nonetheless easy to reach. Many Huron sailors simply put their boats on trailers and drive them to launching ramps along the shore.

The principal base for North Channel cruising is the town of Little Current on pastoral Manitoulin. Anglers may head from there to nearby Bay Finn or McGregor Bay; other mariners explore nearby pine-dotted islets, to pick wild blueberries and often to camp out overnight ashore.

Boatmen setting out into Georgian Bay at the southeastern end of the North Channel can embark at any number of convenient launching spots, such as Parry Sound and Byng Inlet. The most popular destinations are the bays and channels of the Thirty Thousand Islands, where minnows and sunfish make the waters flash, and where three-pound smallmouth bass cruise temptingly.

An early-morning sun casts its reflection in the mirror-smooth waters of McGregor Bay, an area splattered with tiny islets and creased by a maze of narrow channels. Boatmen beware: the bottom is rocky, and depths may vary from 35 feet down to two feet within a few boat lengths. Proceed cautiously, and carry a spare propeller and shaft.

A solitary angler reels in his lure in one of the North Channel's most beautiful fishing holes—The Pool, located at the northeastern end of eight-mile-long Bay Finn. The bay cuts like a narrow fjord between two jutting arms of the Ontario mainland and teems with northern pike, walleye, muskie and black bass. In The Pool and its approaches, water depths are adequate for deep-draft boats, and many mariners anchor there overnight.

Despite the formidable look of these bluffs on its northern end, the harbor of South Benjamin Island near Little Current offers protection in all but southerly winds. Though the northern end shoals off, the mud bottom of the harbor provides good holding ground. The only inhabitants of the pink-tinged granite island, with its inviting coves and gunkholes, are gulls and nonvenomous water snakes.

Lake Erie

Lake Erie, with an average depth of 62 feet, is the shallowest of the Great Lakes. It is also the most industrialized, the most crowded and the most tainted by pollution. But while a campaign to cleanse it gains momentum, the lake encloses pockets of unbesmirched beauty to tempt exploring boatmen.

Most cruising activity centers on a group of 22 islands—13 of them American and nine Canadian—at the western end of the lake where the bottom is generally muddy, but scattered reefs and shallows offer a natural breeding ground for bass, walleye and perch. Part of the islands' charm lies in their descriptive names: Mouse, so dubbed for its diminutive size; Gull, for the birds that nest there; Starve, after a legendary sailor who perished from lack of food on its two acres of rock; Ballast, from whose limestone quarry Commodore Oliver Hazard Perry got ballast for his ships before defeating the British at the Battle of Lake Erie in 1813.

After Perry's triumph, the whole island area remained virtually forgotten until the 1850s, when commercial fishermen arrived seeking whitefish and sturgeon —and when it was also discovered that the islands' limestone soil and mild climate made for excellent grape growing. Today vineyards and wineries lie just beyond the beaches of some of the larger islands, and the heady odor of grapes hangs in the late-summer air.

A boatman who visits the islands will also discover some points of exceptional interest on the mainland nearby. Point Pelee, which is located on the Canadian side, boasts a unique subtropical park. Vermilion, on the Ohio shore, encloses deep lagoons with marinas, yacht clubs, dockside restaurants with their own ships, and a town dock within walking distance of the Great Lakes Historical Society Marine Museum.

A 352-foot granite tower commemorating the American victory in the Battle of Lake Erie dominates the harbor of Put-in-Bay on South Bass Island, Commodore Perry's base of operations against the enemy fleet. By day the monument can be seen for 25 miles; at night the lights at its pinnacle serve as a useful aid to navigation. Put-in-Bay has extensive mooring, docking, fueling and provisioning facilities; however, on some weekends and during the Inter-Lake Regatta in August, boats may have to anchor.

Crystal Cave, one of several subterranean grottoes on South Bass Island, is Put-in-Bay's chief natural attraction. Thirty feet in diameter, it is lined with glistening celestite crystals. Although privately owned, the cave is open to the public; its owners offer tours that include a visit to their nearby winery.

Evidence of the massive glacial forces that created the Great Lakes can be seen in deeply grooved limestone on Kelleys Island near the American mainland. An advancing glacier gouged the pinkish-gray rock about 25,000 years ago, and the tracks were exposed when the ice melted some 12,000 years later. Geology buffs may dock on the south shore, where gas is available, and walk a mile to the grooves; or they can anchor in a protected harbor on the north shore nearer the grooves and row in to a fine sandy beach.

At Old Fort Henry, commissioned by the British during the War of 1812, the crack Fort Henry Guard stages a sunset tattoo twice a week during July and August. The ceremony includes infantry drill, a mock battle and a fife-and-drum concert. The fort, now a military museum, is only a short distance by cab from the harbor at Kingston.

Lake Ontario

Settled since the 18th Century, Lake Ontario retains an air of quiet gentility, from the stately yacht clubs of 200-year-old Toronto in the west to 19th Century Old Fort Henry at Kingston in the northeast. Nowhere is this leisured ambience more evident, or more felicitously combined with cruising fun, than in the Thousand Islands (there are actually about 1,800 of them) at the outlet into the St. Lawrence River. Here, on some of the privately owned islands, sit imposing summer mansions and even an occasional castellated relic from the era of the industrial barons. Scattered between these private demesnes are larger islands supporting villages and farms, or extensive public campgrounds. And at the opposite end of the scale is a plethora of granite knobs so tiny that three birds make a crowd.

Throughout this realm, great blue herons and Canada geese soar over the waters, which teem with perch, black bass, northern pike and 15- to 25-pound muskellunge. A cruising boatman weaves through a labyrinth of channels, some capacious, some barely wide enough to allow a boat to pass.

Visitors to the islands often moor at Gananoque or Alexandria Bay to take a boatman's holiday—an excursion-boat trip to the St. Lawrence Islands National Park and the summer homes of millionaires' row. Then, having hit the high lights, they return to their own vessels to prowl the region's wilder coves and inlets.

Waterborne worshippers are welcome to the interdenominational vesper services held Sundays in July and August at Half Moon Bay on Bostwick Island near Gananoque. The ceremony was born in 1887 when a group of summer campers began to meet in the bay for services; its popularity spread, bringing celebrants of all faiths in boats of all kinds. Today, ushers in canoes paddle among the congregation distributing hymnals.

In the lingering summer twilight, three powerboats have a short stretch of the St. Lawrence River's main channel all to themselves. Much of the time, pleasure craft must share the St. Lawrence with freighters and ore carriers—some measuring 700 feet in length—chugging to and from the port cities of the upper Great Lakes. Whenever commercial vessels are in sight, experienced boatmen stay well clear of the central traffic lane: large ships do not have the maneuvering ability to avoid small craft darting unexpectedly across their bows.

Boldt Castle on Heart Island stands as a monument to the bereavement of the hotel magnate George Boldt. He spent two million dollars on the edifice, which towers over the three-acre heart-shaped island, as a summer home for his bride, Louise. When Louise died suddenly in 1904, the grief-stricken Boldt abandoned the project—still unfinished. Dockage at the island is free, but visitors to the castle pay a small fee to preserve this romantic ruin of a hotelier's dream.

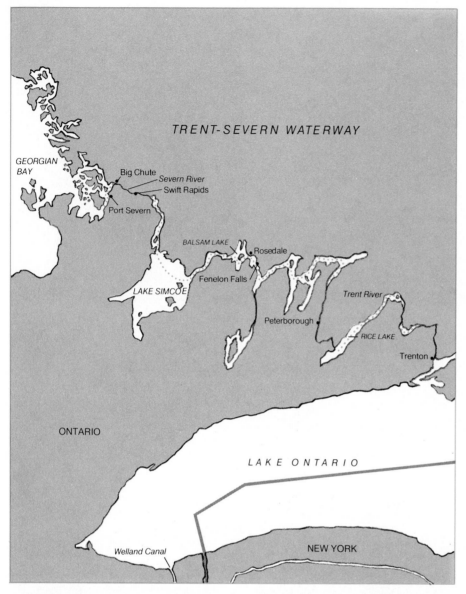

Ontario Passages

When 19th Century entrepreneurs conceived the canal systems that connect Lake Ontario with nearby lakes and rivers, they envisioned the waterways solely as commercial routes. Today, pleasure craft share the Welland and New York State Barge canals with trading vessels, and the Rideau Canal and Trent-Severn Waterway have been given over almost entirely to vacationing mariners.

Showpiece of the system is the Trent-Severn Waterway, which links Lake Ontario with Lake Huron's Georgian Bay. A boatman traveling from west to east enters the canal at Port Severn on Georgian Bay, where he climbs a 58-foot escarpment on a marine railway *(top right)*. Then he glides between the wooded bluffs of the Severn River to emerge into a series of long, meandering lakes loaded with trout, bass, walleye and pike. He continues east along the pastoral Trent River, and by the time he reaches the town of Trenton on Lake Ontario, he has traveled 240 miles, through more than 40 locks—each with its own camping area.

Less bucolic but no less fascinating is the 27-mile-long Welland Canal, which connects Ontario with Lake Erie by a detour around Niagara Falls. The Welland's eight huge electric locks, with a lift of 327 feet, require about 10 hours to negotiate. At the opposite end of Ontario is the 124-mile-long Rideau Canal, which runs north from Kingston near the Thousand Islands to the Canadian capital of Ottawa. In contrast to the mechanized Welland Canal, the Rideau's 47 locks, built between 1826 and 1832, are hand operated.

Longest of Lake Ontario's connecting waterways is the 340-mile New York State Barge Canal, originally christened the Erie Canal. Though it can be entered from the Niagara River at Buffalo, most boatmen prefer to start off from Oswego at Lake Ontario's eastern end *(map, pages 70-71)*, an entryway that provides the most pleasurable cruising—south through Lake Oneida and the lovely Mohawk Valley to the Hudson River at Troy.

Approaching Port Severn on Georgian Bay, an outboard runabout sweeps toward lock 45 at the western end of the Trent-Severn Waterway. At this point the red buoys are kept to port and the black to starboard. But past this first lock the buoy positions reverse, so that red buoys should be left to starboard and the black to port—the standard rule when traveling upstream on the waterway.

A small power cruiser begins a stern-first ascent of the 735-foot-long Big Chute marine railway, eight miles east of Port Severn. The boat has been backed aboard a submerged flatcar and wedged in place. No boat over 50 feet long, or with a draft of more than four feet four inches, or with a beam that exceeds 15 feet, can fit on Big Chute's rails.

Eight miles east of Big Chute railway, a powerboat helmsman approaches lock 43 at Swift Rapids on the Severn River. The yellowish granite rocks and dense stands of pine, spruce, poplar, oak and birch lining the riverbank are characteristic of long stretches of the waterway's wilder western reaches.

ONTARIO PASSAGES: TRENT-SEVERN WATERWAY

A houseboat and two power cruisers move along the waterway at Rosedale, a garden-like resort and popular layover spot near Balsam Lake, the Trent-Severn's highest point. At Rosedale's lock 35, boats start heading downstream toward Lake Ontario, 157 miles to the east. Near the lock, motor courts with their own docks accommodate boatmen who want to splurge overnight on the luxury of a real bed; camper-sailors can pitch tents at campsites on either side of the lock and borrow a washroom key from the lock master.

Boats like this canopied runabout enter and leave lock 34 at Fenelon Falls according to a carefully monitored traffic-control system, typical of many Trent-Severn locks. A television camera atop the standard at the end of the pier warns the lock master of approaching vessels. When a boat is about to leave the lock, as here, the lock master flashes a red signal on the traffic light next to the TV camera, holding back any approaching craft until the lock is clear for entry. Then he turns the light green, giving a go-ahead to the oncoming boat.

Lock 21 at Peterborough on the Trent Canal is the highest hydraulic lift lock in the world. Its twin compartments, each measuring 140 feet by 33 feet, are balanced to raise and lower boats a dizzying 65 feet. As the water level of the chamber at right descends with a cargo of eastbound powerboats heading toward Trenton, the level in the neighboring compartment rises, lifting the houseboat on its way toward Georgian Bay.

Thirteen miles upstream from the beginning of the Trent River, an ancient Indian burial mound rises above the shore of Rice Lake —whose marshes of wild rice formed a rich granary for Indian tribes. Wild rice still grows in abundance in the lake, attracting a profusion of bass and muskellunge; but it can also clog the propellers of any boat that ventures outside the cleared channel.

5 One purple night in 1944, as my PT boat lay at anchor off a palm-fringed South Pacific isle, I was overwhelmed by homesickness. Impressions of my native New England coast kept swimming into my mind. I remembered the salt smell of a cold Maine fog—"thick enough," as down-Easters say, "to cut and stack" —off Machias Bay. And I could almost see the majestic blue bulk of Mt. Desert Island lifting out of the haze of a smoky sou'wester. I savored vicariously the joy of getting into Marblehead early of an afternoon, gliding through a fleet of graceful cruising boats—and then easing into Manchester to moor beside old shipmates and to share whiskey and good talk. I all but

THE NORTHEAST COAST

tasted the bluefish I used to catch as a boy on those diamond-clear days off Connecticut's Thimble Islands. Then and there I solemnly resolved to take any postwar job that offered me a good New England anchorage and time to cruise a coast that affords the best sailing anywhere.

I have since spent the greater part of a lifetime on the coast between New York and Nova Scotia—exploring new anchorages, wandering among tidy little islands, around the long fingers of granite that make up the eastern shoreline's hundreds of peninsulas, poking into quiet inlets alive with wildlife. At the lower end of this superb cruising ground is Long Island Sound, whose south shore embraces dozens of first-class anchorages—though in summer they tend to be crowded. Across the Sound along the Connecticut shore lies a whole necklace of yacht clubs and marinas as well equipped as any in the country. Connecticut also offers beautiful spots for exploration. My own favorites are the Norwalk Islands for a picnic, and then maybe a run up the Connecticut River to East Haddam for a unique evening of Victorian-style dining and play-going at Goodspeed's 1877 Opera House.

The summer winds in the western part of the Sound tend to be a bit flukier than I prefer, but farther east, strong prevailing southwesterlies make for livelier sailing. Fishers Island, New London, Mystic and Stonington are all excellent harbors, and Mystic Seaport, a living museum of maritime history, is an absolute must for anyone who loves the lore of the sea.

East of the Sound sits Block Island, treeless and barren, where some 1,500 boats congregate during Race Week every other June. Ashore are wild berries to pick, fresh swordfish to savor, old hotels with block-long porches, and miles of beaches for swimming, clamming and excellent striped-bass fishing.

For sailors whose tastes are a bit fancier, a half-day's sail north of Block Island lies Newport. The town is rich with golf, tennis, museums, galleries, three or four excellent harbor-front restaurants, and more pre-Revolutionary houses and baronial 19th Century estates than in any other port in America.

From either Newport or Block a sailor can take a day or a month to cruise to Buzzards Bay, the Elizabeth Islands, Nantucket and Martha's Vineyard. I try never to miss Cuttyhunk Island in the Elizabeth group, where the only anchorage is a quarter-mile dredged square and where only early arrivals can count on choice mooring space. Cuttyhunk was where a small Elizabethan bark was wrecked in 1602—an event that inspired Shakespeare's play *The Tempest*. And, like Prospero's Isle, Cuttyhunk has both a fresh- and a salt-water pond, a hill and the very shrubs the playwright mentioned. To me it is a very special place, both for fantasies and for just messing about. I like to take a dinghy to the low-tide beach on the west side of the salt pond to dig for clams. After dining on the haul, I climb the hill and watch the running lights of the last arrivals round the approach buoys and filter into the anchorage.

The Vineyard, to the east, has a quartet of fine harbors, each of them backed by a settlement with a unique character—from tiny Menemsha with

Marblehead, the boating capital of Massachusetts' North Shore, has six yacht clubs, anchorage for 2,000 craft, and the liveliest small-boat racing program in New England.

Veteran Yankee yachtsman Norris Hoyt has spent a lifetime cruising the Atlantic coast, from the Canadian Maritime Provinces to the tip of Florida. When not sailing aboard his 41-foot sloop, Telltale 2, Hoyt lectures on boating and writes for yachting magazines.

its artists and fishermen to very social Edgartown. If you like bicycling, as I do, you can rent a bike and spend a few marvelous hours pedaling the by-ways overlooking the sea. Nantucket, across Nantucket Sound, is smaller, farther out to sea and full of its whaling past. Like the Vineyard, it is a good place to rent a two-wheeler—and also a fine spot to dine. When they're running, the bluefish and striper are superb.

Cape Cod sits above Nantucket like an arm bent at the elbow. Inside the elbow is the great sweep of Massachusetts Bay, most conveniently reached by cutting through the 15-mile-long Cape Cod Canal at the head of Buzzards Bay. Or you can take the deep-water passage along the Cape's Atlantic side, past 50 miles of flawless beaches with no hint of a harbor until Provincetown, inside the Cape's tip—a long, lonely run to challenge the best of sailors. I prefer to go the long way round.

Beyond Cape Cod, however, is the cruising ground that I cherish above all others: the coast of Maine. The water is clear, the shores have great clamming and musseling, and the harborside docks are often groaning with lobster and herring—and plenty of free nautical advice for the wayfarer. The snug bays and pine-clad islands make for spectacular scenery—and cozy refuges when the northeast storms blow up near summer's end. In 20 years of cruising—anchoring every other day in a harbor new to me—I have barely begun to explore the estuaries and back pockets of Maine's bays.

Every lover of this coast has his own private itinerary. For me it starts with a visit to a working port like Cundys Harbor in Casco Bay. Then I work east around Cape Small, past Five Islands and through the racing current of Goose Rock Passage into clean, secluded Robinhood Cove. There I like to savor the resinous morning air as the fog dissipates into a sunny forenoon with a good sailing breeze. I head east next through Townsend Gut and put in at Boothbay Harbor with its artsy-craftsy boutiques, massive powerboat marinas, earth lovers playing guitars and plain folks who have come from the offshore islands for a day of shopping. A superb adventure, but it reaches along only a quarter of the Maine coast.

My own favorite Maine bay is Blue Hill. When the wind is just right, I like to glide into the bay under spinnaker in the dying air of a dry afternoon and make for a patch of green lawn and a pleasant house until a black buoy appears. Then I creep along the shore, passing between the large rocks at the harbor entrance and the larger rocks of the shore to anchor off the one-story yacht club. As the wind begins to die and the fragrance of pine trees creeps down the hillside, Blue Hill itself blots out the sinking sun, and friends arrive with a car to take me to town. There the lawns are wide, the streets overarched by elms, and early-19th Century houses climb hills in all directions. The local general store sells everything—including that epitome of civilization, Earl Grey tea by the pound.

Sometimes, even after I have accepted Maine's invitations, the northern horizon still beckons, and I work up the Bay of Fundy to make a day's run on to St. John, New Brunswick. The river there is navigable for 100 winding miles. But its tides thunder in and out at an awesome 10 knots, creating reversing salt-water rapids at the entrance; a sailor must time his entrance so that it coincides with the dead slack of the tide. From here I move across Fundy to Digby and Yarmouth in Nova Scotia, sneak around Cape Sable and cruise up the coast. Above Halifax the harbors are fewer, leaner and deeper from the sea. At the top of Nova Scotia is one particular spot that never ceases to draw me: the almost totally landlocked Bras d'Or salt-water lakes. The water in them is warmer than the adjacent ocean, and along their shores are scores of primitive, deserted anchorages and two very nice towns, St. Peter's and Baddeck. Like eastern Maine, this is fog country and not for everyone; the stretches are long, the currents strong; the challenges many. For me, it's nothing short of magnificent.

by Norris D. Hoyt

Standing at the eastern gateway to Rhode Island's Narragansett Bay, Newport is the grand dame of New England yachting ports: site of the America's Cup races since 1930, and start of the Bermuda Race. Mansions like Cornelius Vanderbilt's 70-room limestone cottage, The Breakers, sprawl along the ocean front. Well inside the bay, past the city's marinas and commercial wharves, is a jigsaw puzzle of natural and man-made harbors, with first-rate clamming and oyster fishing.

Gift from the Glaciers

From Cape Breton Island in Canada southwest to New York's Long Island, the Atlantic coast presents a ragged profile of harbors, inlets, peninsulas and islands. Geologists call it a drowned land, meaning that glaciers once lay heavy here, pressing the earth's elastic crust downward until the sea penetrated deep into its valleys and scoured its rocky shores.

Pleasure-boaters call it a perfect place to cruise. The coast is 700 miles long as the gull flies, but a sailor with all the time in the world and a shallow draft boat would find it more than 10,000 miles from stem to stern if he were to trace its shoreline. Within this enormous cruising ground lie four distinct sailing areas, each with its unique landscape and seascape, and with its own distinctive wind and weather patterns.

The Atlantic Maritime Provinces of Canada are lusty, salt-drenched and dramatic, with heroic tides and fogs that swirl about their rugged shoreline. The myriad bays of Maine are mazes of granite headlands and protective island chains, all misty pastels in the first foggy warmth of July, sparkling in blues and greens and rocky pinks in the full heat of August.

Cape Cod is a peninsula of glacial debris, its superb beaches the final result of centuries of abrasion of rocks and stones by the sea. So, too, are the low offshore islands of Nantucket Sound and Buzzards Bay. Long Island Sound is an inland sea whose basin marks the farthest advance of the great glaciers. The Sound's 1,500 square miles of protected, sun-warmed waters wash between the river-braided shore of Connecticut on the north and the great sea barrier of Long Island, whose own southern beaches stretch 100 miles from Jones Beach State Park in the west to Montauk in the east.

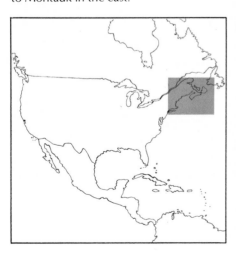

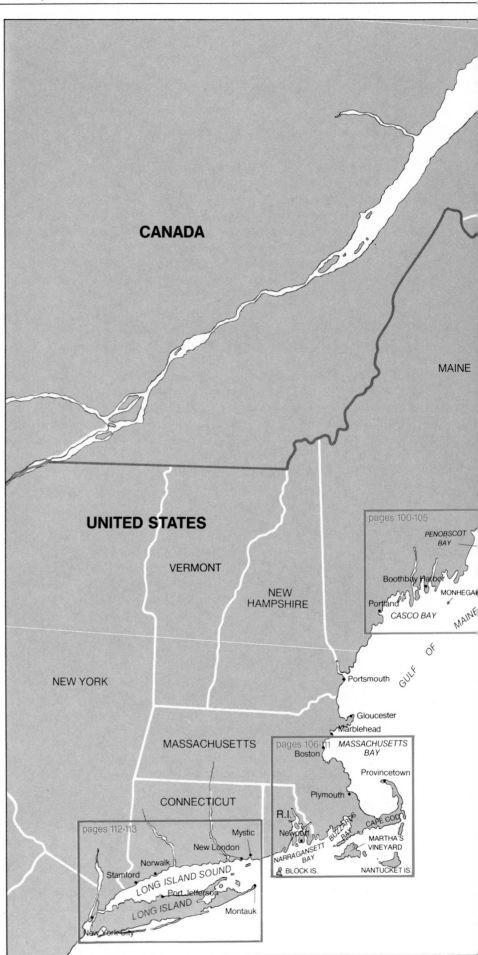

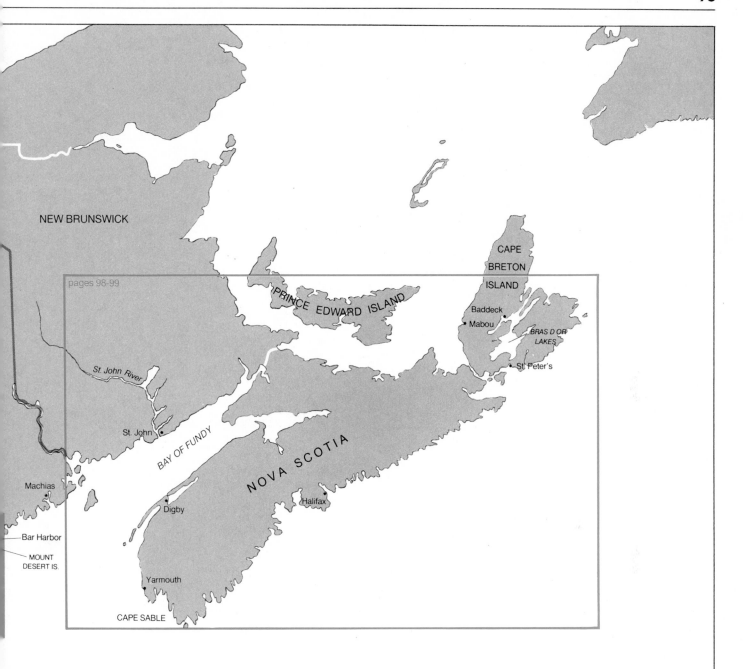

NEW BRUNSWICK

CAPE
BRETON
ISLAND

pages 98-99

PRINCE EDWARD ISLAND

Baddeck
Mabou

BRAS D'OR
LAKES

St Peter's

St. John River

St. John

BAY OF FUNDY

NOVA SCOTIA

Machias

Digby

Halifax

Bar Harbor

MOUNT
DESERT IS.

Yarmouth

CAPE SABLE

ATLANTIC OCEAN

Miles
0   50   100

Winds and Weather

The comfortable season for cruising in New England waters extends from June through September, with a somewhat shorter range north of Cape Cod and up into Canada. Average daily maximum temperatures for the Long Island Sound cruising area are: June 77°, July 83°, August 81° and September 75°. In eastern Maine and Nova Scotia the same months average about 12° cooler. Fog can be expected along the coasts of Maine and Nova Scotia about 14 days a month in the summer. Fog becomes progressively less troublesome as the mariner moves south; Long Island Sound averages a modest two to three days per month.

Prevailing summer winds all along the Northeast Coast come from the southwest. Except for Long Island Sound, where winds typically moderate to less than eight knots in July and August, lively breezes of 10 knots or better can be expected most days, with velocities dropping at sundown as the land cools. Northwest winds, when they come, may provide crystal-clear days and some of the best cruising conditions. East winds almost always presage a siege of rain. Turbulent weather, when it builds, blows in on a northeaster. And thunderstorms, with winds of 35 to 50 knots, sometimes hit Long Island Sound and Massachusetts Bay.

Tides and Currents

Tides in lower New England—Long Island Sound and Massachusetts—range between one and a half and nine feet. But as the boatman moves north, they begin to build. Eleven to 15 feet is not uncommon in eastern Maine; in some river estuaries, they can run as high as 20 feet. Still more extraordinary are the tides in the Bay of Fundy, which average 35 feet in the upper reaches; under certain lunar and solar conditions they have been known to rise as high as 53 feet. Fundy tides also create swift currents.

The region's broad tidal range produces currents of up to five knots in many more southern locales as well. Among the most notorious are Hell Gate, the merging of New York's East and Harlem rivers; The Race, the three-and-one-half-mile-wide eastern entrance to Long Island Sound; and Quicks, Robinsons and Woods Holes in and around the Elizabeth Islands.

Pilotage

The Northeast's ragged coastline presents a complex assortment of underwater hazards—untold thousands of rocks, ledges, isolated shoals and shifting sand bars. Happily, the region is well marked; more than 1,500 major beacons, lights, buoys, Texas Towers and RDF stations are entered in the light list for the area.

Submerged rocks and ledges proliferate along the deep indentations of the Maine and Nova Scotia coasts, so that a pilot must constantly check his position on the chart. Shifting sand shoals off the southern tip of Nova Scotia at Cape Sable—combined with notorious fogs—make this area particularly hazardous.

Between Cape Elizabeth and Cape Ann in Massachusetts, the outlying dangers—mainly rocky islets—are well marked. The shores of Cape Cod are mostly sandy, with sand shoals along the east coast extending well out to sea. Most mariners avoid the outside passage around the Cape and Nantucket, and instead cut south through the 15-mile Cape Cod Canal.

Severe shoaling extends north of Block Island; it should be given at least a half-mile berth. A cluster of underwater rocks extending across The Race at the entrance to Long Island Sound is sufficiently deep to be no threat to most small craft, but the shoals in adjoining Fisher's Island Sound are a constant danger. Inside Long Island Sound, the Connecticut shore is ragged and rock-strewn; however, the main channel is straight and clear, as is the water just off Long Island.

Fishing and commercial shipping create a hazard from Nova Scotia south. Marine traffic is heavy between Cape Cod and the western end of Long Island. Around New London, the U.S. government's biggest submarine base, boatmen also face the peril of finding themselves near suddenly surfacing submarines.

Boats and Special Equipment

The Northeast offers excellent conditions for both power and sailing vessels, with frequent fueling stations and generally steady winds. Well-protected areas such as Long Island Sound, Narragansett Bay and Buzzards Bay can be explored in light-displacement boats, but for coastwise passages across open water, larger and heavier craft are strongly recommended.

Depth gauges and radio direction finders are essential equipment for all boatmen cruising the Northeast. A VHF radio receiver will pick up marine weather broadcasts transmitted on 161.65 mHz frequency in Canada, and on 162.55 or 162.40 mHz in the United States. A Danforth anchor will provide plenty of holding power in the muddy and sandy bottoms west of Cape Cod; but a kedge with narrow flukes is the best security for the hard and rocky ground along the Maine and Nova Scotia coasts.

Wildlife

Great varieties of sea birds abound in the region. The Maritime Provinces provide nesting grounds for puffins, murres, kittiwakes, gannets, herring gulls and eider ducks. Farther south are bald eagles, ospreys, cormorants and great blue herons—and some five species of gulls. Sea mammals include dolphins and porpoises. Mariners in Canada and Maine often spot harbor seals taking the sun on tide-exposed reefs. And a lone deer, caribou or moose can sometimes be seen near the water's edge.

Sports

Northeast waters offer a full menu of game fish and bottom fish. Game-fishing centers are to be found at Yarmouth, Nova Scotia; Bailey Island, Maine; in Massachusetts at Cuttyhunk and at Menemsha on Martha's Vineyard; at Block Island; and at Greenport, Montauk and Patchogue on Long Island. The largest sport fish is Nova Scotia's giant tuna, which weigh up to 1,000 pounds. Farther south are swordfish, striped bass, mackerel and bluefish. Among the bottom fish are flounder, weakfish, pollock, sole, halibut, fluke and cod—the state emblem of Massachusetts.

No licenses are needed for salt-water fishing in U.S. or Canadian waters. For shellfish, especially clams, most states require a license and restrict the size of the haul. (In tidal flats near urban centers, pollution makes clams and mussels bad risks.)

The principal restriction on swimming is the temperature of the water. North and east of Cape Cod, the water can be a chilly 55°, even in August. But elsewhere, along shores warmed by the Gulf Stream, pleasant air and water temperatures ranging from 65 to 75° in summer make for excellent swimming.

Regional Boating Regulations

Boats and marine equipment that meet U.S. Coast Guard standards can be operated legally in the waters of the Maritime Provinces. Customs offices are located all along the coast at such main ports as Yarmouth, Halifax and Sydney. Upon returning to U.S. waters a vessel must be cleared by U.S. customs authorities at one of the official ports of entry listed in the *Coast Pilots,* such as Eastport, Jonesport or Bar Harbor.

Some Canadian boating regulations are far stiffer than those in the United States. For example, Canada requires that all vessels other than rowboats carry, maintain and use the appropriate corrected and up-to-date charts, tide tables, lists of lights, sailing directions, code of navigation practices and procedures, information bulletin, the annual edition of *Canadian Notices to Mariners,* and *Radio Aids to Mariner Navigation* where appropriate. When cruising in the Maritime Provinces, it is customary to fly the Canadian ensign from the starboard spreader or jack staff, although the custom varies locally.

Major Provisioning Ports

This coast, accustomed to generations of seafarers and their needs, is studded with cities and towns where a cruising skipper can expect to find a wide range of goods and services. A sampling of ports with full boating facilities, listed from northeast to southwest, follows:

Baddeck: The chief town and the main point for supplies when cruising the Bras d'Or Lakes on Cape Breton Island.

Halifax: The provincial capital of Nova Scotia, with a fine deepwater harbor, yacht clubs and marinas; a natural provisioning base for cruises throughout the Maritime Provinces.

Bar Harbor: Maine's easternmost resort on Mt. Desert Island; its shops, hotels, restaurants and full marine services make it a superb base camp for expeditions east to Nova Scotia or west along the Maine coast.

Boothbay Harbor: A fishing and boat-building community that offers a convenient layover spot, located midway between Maine's Casco and Muscongus bays.

Portsmouth: New Hampshire's principal port, just across the Piscataqua River from Kittery, Maine, with a handsome, restored waterfront area.

Gloucester: A major fishing port on the north shore of Massachusetts Bay and a convenient departure point for cruises south to Cape Cod.

Padanarum: A favorite layover spot in Buzzards Bay, with two marine yards. The harbor is only a short bus ride to the ship hardware stores and supermarkets of New Bedford.

Newport: The chief supply point for yachts sailing Rhode Island's Narragansett Bay, and a natural jumping-off place for boats headed east to Martha's Vineyard or west to Block Island.

New London: A fine harbor of refuge on the east end of Long Island Sound, with a submarine base and shipyards.

Port Jefferson: A virtually landlocked harbor on the southern shore of Long Island Sound with ample dock spaces.

Stamford: Western Connecticut's largest port, and a good place to begin cruises into the Sound, with six boatyards and six yacht clubs and the largest marina in the Northeast.

City Island: New York City's headquarters for yacht building and repair, and the westernmost provisioning center on Long Island Sound.

Coast Guard Stations

The Canadian Coast Guard operates lifeboat stations in Nova Scotia at Fishermans Harbour, Clarks Harbour and Westport, and a cutter patrol from Dartmouth. In addition, the Ministry of Transport maintains a Rescue Co-ordination Centre at Halifax. The First Coast Guard Division, based in Boston, covers the coastal waters and tributaries from Maine to the western end of Rhode Island with a total of 23 stations. The Third Coast Guard Division covers Rhode Island through New York from headquarters at Governors Island, New York, with 15 stations.

Charts and Publications

The general area is covered by U.S. National Ocean Survey chart 13006 and Canadian chart 4003, by Volume I of the light lists, by Marine Weather Service Charts MSC-1, Eastport, Maine to Montauk Point, New York, and MSC-2, Montauk Point to Manasquan, New Jersey, and also by the East Coast tide tables. Piloting information can be found in *Nova Scotia (S.E. Coast) and Bay of Fundy Sailing Directions* and in *United States Coast Pilot 1, Atlantic Coast, Eastport to Cape Cod* and *Coast Pilot 2, Cape Cod to Sandy Hook.* Tidal current charts are available for Boston Harbor, Narragansett Bay to Nantucket Sound, Narragansett Bay, Block Island Sound and Eastern Long Island, and Long Island Sound and Block Island Sound. To locate the applicable sailing and harbor charts, consult the NOS *Nautical Chart Catalog 1* and *Canadian Nautical Charts, Bulletin 14.* Slight variations will appear in the two chart series. Up-to-date chart revisions are available in major ports or they can be obtained from the appropriate government agencies that follow:

Defense Mapping Agency Depot
5801 Tabor Avenue
Philadelphia, Pennsylvania 19120

National Ocean Survey
Distribution Division, C44
6501 Lafayette Avenue
Riverdale, Maryland 20840

Hydrographic Chart Distribution Office
Department of the Environment
1675 Russell Road
Ottawa, Ontario, Canada, K1A0E6

The most reliable piloting and cruising guides for this area are:

Bartlett, Charles W., ed., *Cruising Guide to the Nova Scotia Coast.* Boston: Cruising Club of America, Royal Nova Scotia Yacht Squadron.

Boating Almanac. Morristown, N.J.: Boating Almanac Co.

Duncan, Roger F., and John P. Ware, *A Cruising Guide to the New England Coast.* New York: Dodd, Mead & Company.

Eldridge Tide and Pilot Book. Boston: Robert Eldridge White.

Lund, Morten, *Cruising the Maine Coast.* New York: Walker & Co.

Waterway Guide, Northern Edition. Annapolis, Maryland: Marine Annuals, Inc.

Wilensky, Julius M., *Long Island Sound.* Stamford, Conn.: Snug Harbor Publishing Co.

The Maritime Provinces

The peninsula of Nova Scotia advances boldly into the Atlantic Ocean like a shield protecting the Canadian mainland. Like the other two Maritime Provinces, New Brunswick and Prince Edward Island, Nova Scotia is remote, with an austere beauty—delightful cruising territory for anyone sure of his skills as a navigator.

Nova Scotia's Atlantic shore is generously supplied with small, snug harbors every few miles and has a moderate tidal range of four feet. The fog, however, is anything but moderate. Sailors can expect 10 to 14 days of pure pea soup every month in summer.

The northwesterly shore, back in the Bay of Fundy, draws fewer pleasure boats, though its spectacular highlands tend to dispel the fog. The hazard here is the tidal range, which measures up to 50 feet in places and generates currents of up to five knots. Beyond Digby (right) there are no anchorages at low water. Every harbor simply becomes a vast red-bottomed mud flat, and only powerboat owners and local fishing boats venture this way.

Perhaps the most intriguing and least hazardous cruising venue in all Nova Scotia lies to the east on Cape Breton Island, politically part of Nova Scotia but separated from it by the Strait of Canso. Deep within the island and accessible from north and south are the salt-water Bras d'Or Lakes. Here, bald eagles soar, caribou come down to the water's edge, and the cruising man can savor 450 square miles of wild and splendid sailing ground.

Digby's waterfront in late afternoon is choked with draggers home from a day's scallop fishing. Yachtsmen can tie up overnight at an L-shaped government dock nearby. But as the tidal range here can go to 25 feet, special care should be taken with shorelines.

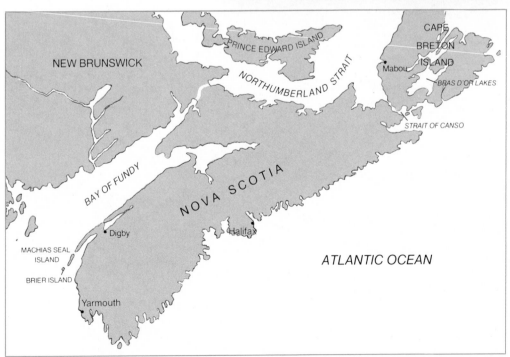

Basalt columns rising 1,000 feet above the sea mark the southwest face of Brier Island in the Bay of Fundy. Though this raw coast has no harbors, adventurous yachtsmen can sail to the more protected east coast and go ashore among wild flowers and sea birds.

The emerald pastures of Mabou, a tiny Cape Breton settlement, sweep down to the scalloped shore of Northumberland Strait. Though there are open anchorages like the one inside the sandspit above, the only protected spot along a 75-mile stretch of Cape Breton's northwest shore is Mabou Harbor, a mile south. Even there, yachtsmen must enter at slack water to avoid the channel's four-knot current.

Two puffins, their beaks gaudy with the intensified colors of the mating season, eye each other on a promontory atop Machias Seal Island. Once found in great numbers along the coast, these perky sea divers now nest in only a few North Atlantic rookeries.

Down East

Maine's coastline almost seems to have been designed with boatmen in mind, so generous has nature been in strewing their paths with harbors, coves, sheltering islands and scenery of breathtaking beauty. Nature has also provided favorable summer winds to take boats there: centuries ago, sailors noted that a trip from any other part of New England to Maine was almost always downwind, which is why Maine is often referred to as down East.

For cruising purposes, Maine's serrated shoreline can be separated into five segments—each a sizable bay providing ample opportunity for leisurely exploration. The northernmost of these is Frenchman Bay, washing the eastern slopes of Mount Desert Island *(right)*. Blue Hill Bay, to the west, is chock-full of fir-clad islands and almost empty of people. Nearby Penobscot Bay *(pages 102-103)*, 20 miles wide and extending 30 miles inland, is the largest, most varied and most protected of all Maine's cruising grounds.

Muscongus Bay, southwest of Penobscot, is more open to the Atlantic, with adjacent Monhegan Island *(pages 104-105)* providing an offshore lure. The bay itself is studded with towns that got their start as shipbuilding ports—notably Thomaston, home of fine whaling ships, and Friendship, where shipwrights still produce a sturdy sloop that began coming down the ways in the 1880s. Maine's last major bay, Casco, to the west, has a happenstance distinction all its own: the bay embraces a total of 365 islands—one for every day in the year.

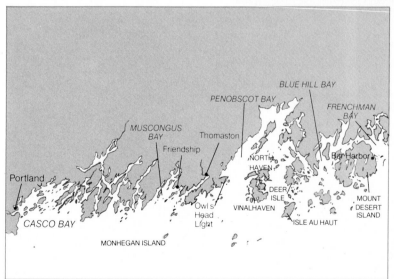

Boring 82 feet into Mount Desert's granite-bound coast, Anemone Cave breeds a remarkable colony of sea anemones—bright-colored relatives of jellyfish and coral.

MOUNT DESERT ISLAND

On a clear day the view from atop barren Cadillac Mountain, on Mount Desert Island, embraces the century-old summer resort of Bar Harbor to the island-bespattered waters of Frenchman's Bay and Schoodic Peninsula on the mainland beyond. At 1,530 feet, Cadillac is the loftiest summit on the U.S. Atlantic coast and the crowning feature of Acadia National Park. The park encompasses about half of the island's 150 square miles, plus large portions of nearby Isle au Haut and Schoodic Peninsula. Founded in 1919, it draws over two million visitors a year.

Stark and sometimes storm-tossed, Hunters Head on Mount Desert's southeastern face must be given a wide berth in southwesters. Although the rocky headlands take the full brunt of the Atlantic surf, their stands of spruce hold on to a thin layer of soil and in summer shelter a lush growth of wild cranberries, blueberries and flowers.

Low tide in Penobscot Bay bares the pilings
of a lobsterman's dock at Stonington on Deer
Isle, while the local lobster fleet swings
lazily on moorings in one of three coves that
make up an ample harbor. Although
Stonington now wins its modest living almost
entirely from the sea, the town was—as the
name suggests—a quarrying center in the late
1800s and exported handsome pink granite
for use in libraries and statehouses all
up and down the East Coast.

Owl's Head Light at the southwest entrance
to Penobscot Bay has been sending out its
beam since 1826, when it was built to guide
merchantmen en route to the shipbuilding
port of Bangor up the Penobscot River.
Perched 80 feet up on a promontory crowned
with evergreens, the light can be seen on a
clear night from 16 miles away.

The Fox Island Thoroughfare between North Haven and Vinalhaven islands offers a secure, secluded all-weather anchorage for pleasure-boaters cruising Penobscot Bay. These two islands (once known jointly as the Fox Islands because of the silver foxes that roamed there) first prospered in the 1870s, when great schools of mackerel appeared in nearby waters. Although the fish soon moved on as mysteriously as they had come, the islands continued to thrive as a fashionable retreat for summer rusticators from Boston and New York, whose rambling estates line the thoroughfare's two shores.

A Penobscot lobsterman uses a bronze lobster gauge to make sure that his catch measures up to the legal standard. Shorts —lobsters less than three and three sixteenths inches from eye socket to the end of the carapace—are thrown back to their rocky lairs to grow some more. Maine lobsters are generally held to be the world's tastiest— and they can often be bought from a lobster boat at well below the market price.

Heading out from Monhegan's narrow harbor, a cruising sloop squeezes between a mooring post and a lobster boat moored in the lee of Manana Island. The harbor, best entered from the north, is frequently crowded in summer, when pleasure craft share space with Monhegan's 13-boat lobster fleet; visitors can anchor in 15 feet of water in a rocky bottom or tie up to one of several mooring buoys.

DOWN EAST: MONHEGAN ISLAND

The prospect west from the 140-foot central hilltop of Monhegan Island reveals the main village of trim shingle dwellings and the island's only anchorage in the channel between the town and low-lying Manana Island. Doggedly traditional in outlook, the islanders have neither paved roads nor a central electrical system. But cruising yachtsmen will find supplies at Monhegan's general store and sturdy New England fare at the tables of Island Inn, the 19th Century structure that dominates the village.

A freshly painted picket fence sets off a pair of roomy summer cottages, brightening a typically fogbound morning. While summer fogs often roll out by noon, the fog in winter may settle in as though for good, sometimes accompanied by severe northeast storms.

NANTUCKET ISLAND

Nantucket's harbor, a shallow lagoon extending nearly five miles behind the scalloped sand barrier of Coatue Point on the island's northwestern flank, was home to over 100 ships and thousands of seamen in the 1760s. Today, sailors will find generous mooring facilities and an excellent marina close by the town's shopping district.

Of Nantucket's many old houses—and there are more than 800 dating from before 1840 —none are more celebrated than the "Three Bricks," a trio of nearly identical private houses built between 1836 and 1838 by whale-oil merchant Joseph Starbuck for his sons. Set just back from a cobbled Main Street in the manner of London row houses, the Three Bricks reflect the town's early ambitions to become a "city at sea."

The Yankee Islands

Although Nantucket, Martha's Vineyard, Block Island and the islands in the Elizabeth chain are geological siblings, all spawned in the same glacial era, each is distinct in appearance and ambience.

Nantucket lies farthest out in the Atlantic, 25 miles south of Cape Cod, behind a barricade of shifting sand shoals. Once it was the capital of New England's lucrative whaling industry, its name and its citizens known in port cities all over the world. Today the island of Nantucket lives with its heritage still intact, but with an overlay of summer chic that makes it a haven for tennis players, bicyclers, surfers, antique-hunters and gourmets—as well as just plain pleasure-boaters.

Martha's Vineyard, 12 miles to the west, is a somewhat larger island, with four markedly different harbors: Edgartown, with its fine yacht club, shallow Oak Bluffs, the fishing port of Menemsha and Vineyard Haven, with a marine railway for repairs. Visiting boaters will find much on shore to amuse them, from boutiquing in Edgartown to Saturday night band concerts in Oak Bluffs.

The Elizabeth Islands, strung out in a line separating Buzzards Bay from Vineyard Sound, are 16 in number, and all but two of them are privately owned. Except for Cuttyhunk Island they offer no services, but together they form a deliciously serene area for dropping anchor, bird-watching and just plain unwinding.

Block Island rises in splendid isolation some 12 miles out to sea from mainland Rhode Island. With few trees and a high land mass measuring about 18 square miles, it is rarely without wind. Its structures, boldly silhouetted against rolling green moors, are a mixture of grandiose Victorian and down-to-earth farmhouses, most of them now summer homes for a seasonal population. Sport fishing, especially for swordfish, is the local passion.

The Old Mill, sited on a hilltop overlooking the town of Nantucket, was built in 1746, partly from timbers of a ship wrecked off the island. The only survivor among five mills that once stood here, it has been lovingly restored by local historians. From time to time canvas sails are lashed to the vanes, the wind sets them turning, and cornmeal is ground—and sold to the islanders—as of old.

Beach grass and snow fences to hold dunes in place are Nantucket's first line of defense against the sea. Its 55 miles of sandy shore are enough to provide swimming, surf casting and solitude for everyone. Nantucket's unusually warm waters—72° in August, as compared to the chill Cape waters—are caused by the Gulf Stream's proximity.

THE YANKEE ISLANDS: MARTHA'S VINEYARD

Menemsha, on the western end of Martha's Vineyard, makes only a few concessions to the yachtsman. Dockside slips at the harbor basin, close by the channel shown at right, are often crowded. And the waterfront offers no more than a cluster of small tackle and bait shops for fishermen. But a mile south along the channel, Menemsha Pond provides a placid refuge for both yachtsmen and an extraordinary variety of shore birds —antipollution laws require all boats to be equipped with holding tanks for sewage.

Gay Head, the westernmost point on the Vineyard, has been a familiar landfall for New England sailors for centuries. The first of two lighthouses was constructed here in 1799. Even before that, its terra-cotta, yellow and tan cliffs provided a showy landmark by day —and were once the source of clay for a thriving pottery industry among the Wampanoag Indians. Gay Head offers no anchorage, but it is a wonderfully isolated picnic ground and is reachable either on foot or by taxi from nearby Menemsha.

A whaling port in the 1800s, a summer resort since the 1890s, Edgartown today is a nice mix of early history, old gentility and modern sailing. Handsome cottages and handsomer boats are much in evidence along the harbor, which affords good shelter from all but northeasterly blows. But skippers should read their charts carefully to find adequate holding ground—away from the hard sand bottom and fearsomely swift tide of the channel, and onto the mud.

Filled to capacity, Edgartown's inner harbor takes on festive colors with the annual visit of the large New York Yacht Club fleet. Though the visitors' schedule changes slightly every year, they generally take a layover day here to enjoy the town's hospitality. Another regular salt-water event at Edgartown is the annual regatta, a three-day event held late in July featuring an overnight round-the-island race.

Second largest of the Elizabeth Islands, Nashawena provides this sheltered anchorage in a setting of meadowland and sparkling white beaches. Nearby, between Nashawena and Pasque, is Quicks Hole, the principal passage for boats crossing between Buzzards Bay and Vineyard Sound. All the islands in the chain, save Cuttyhunk, a resort, and Penikese, a bird sanctuary, are privately owned. Though yachtsmen may land, they are asked not to go beyond the beaches.

The gaff-rigged schooner Bill of Rights, with charterers off on a cruise, churns across Great Salt Pond on Block Island. A mile long and nearly as wide, the pond is almost entirely landlocked; its only opening to the sea is a narrow channel on its western shore. Thus protected from virtually all directions, the pond provides a superb anchorage for up to 500 boats. Another, smaller anchorage next to town is Old Harbor, a port of refuge for commercial fishing boats.

Long Island Sound

Long Island Sound, extending about 125 miles between the nearly parallel shores of Connecticut and Long Island, is one of the busiest boating areas of its size in the world. Its flanks provide berthing places for an estimated 250,000 registered pleasure craft, plus uncounted thousands of skiffs, commercial vessels and unregistered sailboats. The Sound's popularity is due in part to the great urban concentrations of people living nearby. But more significantly, this inland sea comes close to perfection as a protected deepwater recreational area, with generally clement weather for five months of the year, varied scenery, excellent harbors, and fine swimming and sport fishing.

The Sound's two shores offer distinctly different environments for laying over. The Connecticut side is rocky and tree-lined, with a scattering of small islands close to shore providing added shelter to many of its small harbors. Its beaches are few and often privately maintained, but the numerous yacht clubs—some redolent of 19th Century boating tradition —are hospitable to boats flying other club pennants. Several navigable rivers emptying along this shore offer diverting side trips for sailors, most especially the Connecticut River, with the lovely old town of Essex six miles upstream, and Mystic River with its outdoor museum (top right) near the mouth.

Long Island's shore, by contrast, presents an undulating course of sand hills and spits, many accessible to anyone towing a skiff. This shore also boasts a succession of roomy harbors along its western half, beginning at Little Neck Bay and continuing on to Port Jefferson Harbor (right). From there to Orient Point at the northeastern tip of the island, the shore is an almost impenetrable barrier of sand cliffs—no place for overnighting but a lovely setting for midday stopovers.

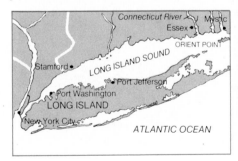

At Mystic Seaport, Connecticut, pleasure boats can reserve overnight dock space among the tall ships of another era at a brilliantly executed outdoor museum of maritime history. Attractions include the ships Joseph Conrad (left) and Charles W. Morgan (right), and a restored 19th Century sea village with sail lofts, a ship chandlery, a rigging loft and a shop that produces carved wooden figureheads.

Mount Misery Cove, just inside Port Jefferson's broad, bustling harbor, is a snug cul-de-sac with good holding ground of up to 18 feet. The bare, 100-foot-high sandy bluffs can be climbed with much slipping and sliding—all part of the fun. Across from Mount Misery and down behind the long arm of Old Field Beach are two more small anchorages: Strong's Neck and the shallower inlet of Conscience Bay.

Sands Point, Long Island, and the sandy cove at its eastern edge (foreground) are just 12 miles from the towers of Manhattan, but as a temporary stop for a swim or picnic, the area is as pleasant as any on the western Sound. Just around the point is Manhasset Bay, a beehive of Long Island boating activities with a host of yacht clubs, marinas and other services, and the populous town of Port Washington.

6 Every year an extraordinary seasonal migration of boats, some 10,000 vessels strong, moves along the 900-mile chain of protected waterway between Florida and the mid-Atlantic cruising grounds. I have joined the migration many times, starting south in the fall from the canal that links the upper reaches of the Chesapeake and Delaware bays, and heading north again in spring from the Florida border. Typical of migrants, most skippers on the waterways travel as fast as possible; auxiliaries push along at up to 60 miles a day, and powerboats at 140. But for me, a Yankee with the chill of Maine nor'easters in my bones, these waterways are places to linger—a revelation of rivers, creeks,

THE MID-ATLANTIC WATERWAYS

antebellum cities, sandspits, gunkholes, pine islands, wildlife refuges and some of the best regional cooking in all North America.

Chesapeake Bay, at the western end of the Chesapeake and Delaware Canal, is so intriguing to me that whenever I enter it I am tempted to go no farther. The bay reaches 190 miles into the Maryland-Virginia coast, measures about 20 miles across at its widest and has over 5,000 miles of shoreline. Forty rivers flow into it, and though the bay is notoriously shallow in spots, it offers over 230 good harbors. The eating is fabulous, the tide is negligible, the marinas numerous—and, for me, the ambiance unsurpassed among U.S. cruising grounds. The Chesapeake's Eastern Shore is awash with gentlemen farmers, duck hunters, fishermen and prosperous retirees, its landscape scattered with relics of plantation-era living. The Western Shore is cities, yacht clubs, national monuments and battlefields—from star-spangled Fort McHenry near the head of the bay to Yorktown near the mouth.

My advice to any novitiate is to take two weeks for your first cruise, and start near the top by running up the Sassafras River to Georgetown for supplies and great dining. Then, if you are cruising in a sailboat, reach across to the Western Shore and spend the night in Gibson Island's perfect harbor. Next, reach back again to the Chester River, turning into Queenstown Creek to drop anchor at the little harbor inside. By now you will have learned two of the basic tenets of sailing the Chesapeake: (1) always reach across the wind to the next harbor; (2) every harbor has another harbor tucked inside it.

Cast off early next morning for Annapolis. You'll need most of the day to explore the old State House where George Washington handed in his commission at the end of the Revolution, and to see the U.S. Naval Academy and a bountiful assemblage of other historic buildings. Next, cross again to the Eastern Shore at St. Michaels or Oxford—or take an extra day to visit both. The former has a maritime museum and a handsome waterfront; the latter boasts a great harbor and enough hospitable people to populate a state.

As you zigzag down the bay, be sure to put in at Tangier Island. Anchor among the crab floats, and while you negotiate for a mess of crabs, prepare to be an object of great curiosity to Tangier's children, who hang around the waterfront like bees around a hive. From there, go south to the York River; anchor in Sarah Creek and charter a car for a land cruise to the single most historic triangle of towns in America: Yorktown, where Lord Cornwallis surrendered to General Washington; Jamestown, the first permanent English settlement in the New World; and Williamsburg, the elaborate restoration of Virginia's colonial capital. So far you have been 14 days on the inland waterways system, and you've already missed at least 216 elegant harbors. And the cruise has barely started.

Just a long day's sail south in Norfolk is Mile Zero of the waterways system's backbone, the Intracoastal Waterway, that begins in Norfolk's teeming roadstead, full of tugs, tows, piers, crab skiffs, colliers, retired ocean liners,

The port of Annapolis in the northwest corner of Chesapeake Bay boasts three fine harbors, including Spa Creek, shown here, and shelters one of the largest sailboat fleets in the East.

submarines, carriers, radio towers, marinas, bridges, apartment houses, dry docks. Seven miles down the waterway you emerge from all the bustle to glide in a sylvan canal through the Great Dismal Swamp, a delightful stretch of pure wilderness region, despite its lugubrious name.

Let me give you a few of the sensations and memories of a late autumn passage down The Ditch, as the waterway is often called. It is November 25, and we are anchored at Mile 33, South Mills Lock on the Dismal Swamp Canal. The morning's dew is frozen, and as I walk toward the lock keeper's station to rouse him from his morning torpor and coffee, clumps of wild chive break off like icicles under my feet. A warm-water mist rises in crystal air all along the canal as we move on down it. The gum leaves are pure-ruby stars against the velvet of brown water. Migrant ducks, startled by our approach, take off in waves ahead of us, and the water mirrors blue-and-white sky, dark shadows of the black gum, cypress, juniper and white cedar. Here and there mistletoe climbs a poplar. Bear, deer and bobcats lurk in the almost impenetrable jungle that stretches off to starboard.

Our route leads out of the canal on through Albemarle and Pamlico sounds. Starting at Mile 235, we run through a firing range used by Marines from Camp Lejeune. Flocks of egrets nervously wheel inshore, and suddenly we hear the sound of guns. We spot a squad of camouflaged leathernecks, almost invisible under the trees. After a moment a Marine anchored in a skiff near shore signals us that the way is clear, and we throttle ahead.

One day later, at Mile 295, we put in at Carolina Beach's sock-shaped harbor (six feet deep on the chart). We idle on cautiously, depth finder beating in tempo with my nervous heart (we draw six and a half feet). As it turns out, there are 12 feet of water all the way to a good dock. Tying up, we meet two Canadian families who have sold all their land and chattels, bought two 32-foot cutters and are within a week of starting to sail around the world. Thinking of their dreams and their courage, we wander the streets and beaches of this winter-bare resort and then continue our own easy-going adventure.

Barely into South Carolina at Little River (Mile 344), we buy a five-pound king mackerel from a fishing boat fresh in. We bake a third of it and put the rest on ice: fried mackerel for breakfast, chowder for lunch.

Two days later we wake at dawn to a thick sea fog and feel our way between marsh banks and inlets. At Mile 464 we reach Charleston Harbor. Abruptly the fog clears, and the hot sun shows us Fort Sumter behind to port and the spectacle of beautiful Charleston's porticoed, colonnaded waterfront to starboard. Ashore we resist the boutiques of Catfish Row (really Cabbage Row before *Porgy and Bess*) en route to dine in a colonial tavern.

Two days farther on, at Mile 536, in Beaufort, South Carolina, we meet a photographer who says he caught 73 sea trout last Saturday from the deck of his 26-foot sailboat. Now we slide inside the sea islands of South Carolina and Georgia. In past times some of America's richest plantations flourished here. The owners grew indigo, sugar cane, cotton, rice and ship timber. After the Civil War the islands' prosperity faded. Today, parts of the area retain the slumberous tempo of those post-bellum days. We glide past mile after mile of sandspits and marshy wilderness. Some of the land, alas, has been grabbed by developers who put up minimansions on two-acre plots, supermarinas, air taxis and shops for everything.

The last of the Georgia islands, Cumberland, at Mile 690, has been saved from developers and made a federally protected national seashore. We move through waters laced with the nets of shrimp boats, heavily populated by gulls. Pelicans stab the waters, egrets and blue heron stalk the shores, dolphin splash and blow beside the boat, and our first wild alligator dives abruptly. Then we leave this beautiful sanctuary, more primitive than it was in 1800, and cross the St. Marys River into Florida—Fernandina Beach, for us the end of a unique cruising adventure.

by Norris D. Hoyt

The Dismal Swamp Canal—its name belying the eerie beauty of this quiet, tree-lined waterway—cuts 43 miles through dense cypress and juniper swamps to connect Norfolk, Virginia, with Albemarle Sound in North Carolina. Proposed by George Washington in the mid-18th Century and built by slave labor in the early 19th, the canal is the oldest man-made waterway in the Intracoastal system.

The Upper Passage

Part nature's providence, part the work of men, the system of protected waterways that stretches between Delaware Bay and Florida has been providing sailors with safe passage since the Spanish explorer Esteban Gómez poked the prow of his ship in among the Georgia Sea Islands in 1525. The first English settlements in the New World were established along the waterways' shores—on North Carolina's Outer Banks in 1587 and then at Jamestown, Virginia, in 1607. And in 1608 Captain John Smith pronounced the largest single segment, Chesapeake Bay, perfection: "Heaven and earth never agreed better to frame a place for man's habitation."

Efforts to make navigational improvements on nature's good works began in a major way in 1793 at Great Dismal Swamp. There a group of speculators, including Patrick Henry, financed a 22-mile ditch connecting Norfolk on the Chesapeake with Albemarle Sound in North Carolina. In 1829 the Chesapeake was linked at its head to neighboring Delaware Bay via the Chesapeake and Delaware Canal. And in 1856 work began on the 13-mile Virginia Cut as an alternate route to the Dismal Swamp Canal.

Finally, in the 1870s, the federal government took over full responsibility for unifying and otherwise improving what had slowly become a key maritime artery. The Army Corps of Engineers began deepening hundreds of already existing waterway miles and added some of their own. And later the U.S. Coast Guard set up a distinctive buoyage system beginning at Norfolk and heading south. This stretch, formally designated the Intracoastal Waterway, is the system's backbone. With that last project, the mid-Atlantic waterways were completed as they stand today: 1,450 miles of navigable bays, rivers, creeks and sounds, stretching from northern Maryland at the head to Key West, Florida.

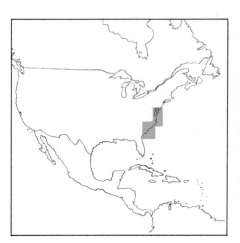

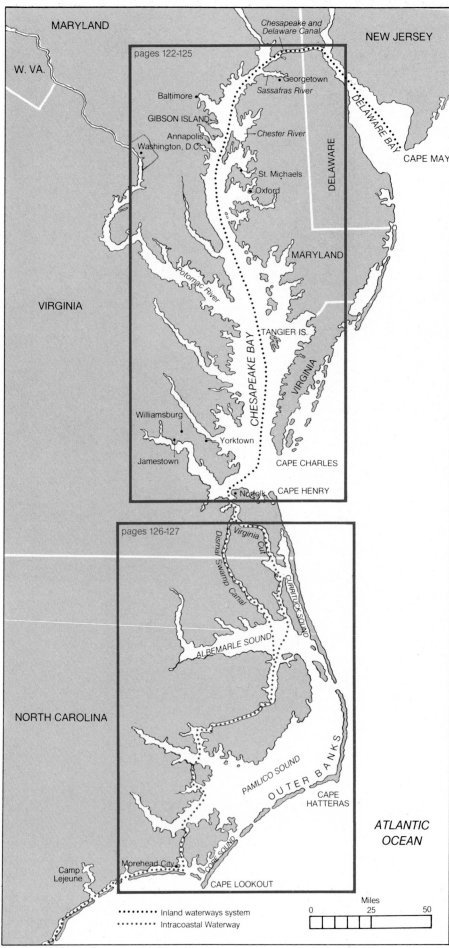

········· Inland waterways system
········· Intracoastal Waterway

Miles
0   25   50

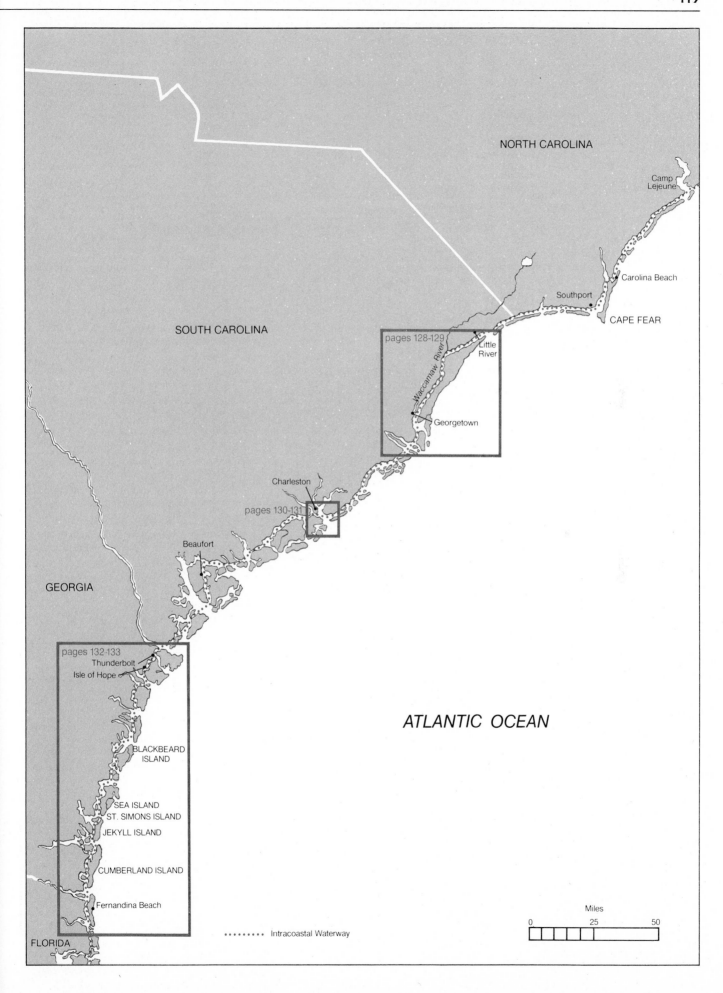

NORTH CAROLINA

Camp Lejeune

Carolina Beach

Southport

CAPE FEAR

SOUTH CAROLINA

pages 128-129

Little River

Waccamaw River

Georgetown

Charleston

pages 130-131

Beaufort

GEORGIA

pages 132-133

Thunderbolt

Isle of Hope

ATLANTIC OCEAN

BLACKBEARD ISLAND

SEA ISLAND
ST. SIMONS ISLAND

JEKYLL ISLAND

CUMBERLAND ISLAND

Fernandina Beach

FLORIDA

·········· Intracoastal Waterway

Miles

0   25   50

Winds and Weather

Weather along the mid-Atlantic waterways is subject to the mix of extremes that characterizes most temperate climates. Calm and steamy summers often bring days of sweltering 90° heat and 80 per cent humidity, with light breezes angling in from the southwest. Then, particularly on Chesapeake Bay, a week of windless heat will erupt in a thundersquall with gale-force winds. Within a half hour after it starts, the squall usually dies down and the heat returns. Winters, in contrast, can be surprisingly cold. Temperatures drop to a daily 40° average between December and March, and chilly northers with 45-knot winds penetrate well below the Florida border.

The best cruising times lie between these seasonal extremes. Spring and autumn bring 70° temperatures and moderate winds of 10 knots or so. Spring is slightly preferable, since the mid-Atlantic coast is in the path of occasional autumn hurricanes, which are no real threat to boatmen who follow National Weather Service reports on VHF-FM channels WX-1 and WX-2.

Tides and Currents

Tides range from less than a foot in Chesapeake Bay and the North Carolina sounds to more than eight feet around the Georgia Sea Islands. Tidal currents generally run at less than two knots throughout the waterway system. One exception is a strong ebb-tide current of four knots that sweeps past Southport on the Cape Fear River in North Carolina. In addition, confusing crosscurrents, running in more than one direction at once, occur where the Intracoastal Waterway traverses a natural stream, or an ocean inlet. In either case, the deeper channel carries the stronger branch of the current. Crosscurrents are especially strong at New River Inlet and Bogue Inlet, North Carolina.

Pilotage

The narrow passageways of the Intracoastal Waterway pose a constant set of unique piloting situations for the cruising skipper. The waterway's path through the myriad channels of the mid-Atlantic region is designated on small-craft charts as a solid magenta line. Out on the water, this channel is marked by a distinctive buoyage system designed to keep the skipper on course as the waterway passes through inlets, harbors, bays and sounds whose channels are marked by conventional buoys of their own. Wherever the Intracoastal intersects another channel, a yellow square or triangle on a navigation aid marks the waterway's course. To stay on the waterway going south, the yellow squares must be left to port and the triangles to starboard *no matter what other markings the aid may carry.*

When passing the Intracoastal's channel markers, the skipper should always give them wide berth—at least 50 feet—since they are often placed in shallower water just outside the main channel. In addition, despite the best efforts of the Army Corps of Engineers' dredges, the waterway channels have a tendency to shoal in at their sides. The skipper should be particularly wary of this shoaling tendency in broad, shallow sounds and near ocean inlets after northeasterly storms. For last-minute reports on conditions in the waterway's channels, boatmen can contact the Operations Division, Army Corps of Engineers, at Baltimore, Maryland; Norfolk, Virginia; Wilmington, North Carolina; Charleston, South Carolina; or Savannah, Georgia.

The waterway is often packed with traffic in both directions. In such two-way traffic, all boats must stay to the right and steer with constant care to avoid collision. A second traffic hazard comes from tugs and motorized barges, whose powerful propellers may kick up debris from the bottom. Tailgating these commercial craft may result in the loss of bottom paint, or even a bent or broken propeller or shaft. To avoid trouble with other vessels in the waterway's close quarters, cruising skippers should carefully read the inland section of the Rules of the Road.

Another potential piloting hazard on the Intracoastal are the numerous bridges across the waterway. Fixed bridges in the mid-Atlantic waterways have a minimum vertical clearance of 65 feet; the high-tide clearances of drawbridges are indicated on charts. Before each day's run, the skipper should mark on his chart any bridge of insufficient clearance he will encounter.

Boats and Special Equipment

Though the Chesapeake offers superb sailing, the Intracoastal Waterway itself is no paradise for sailors. Only about one third of the route from Norfolk to Miami is navigable under sail alone. Sailboats making the trip must be equipped with an auxiliary. An ideal cruising boat is a 30- to 40-foot diesel trawler type. Enough accommodation for comfort can be wedged into the hull without making the boat cumbersome, and the diesel engine provides reliable, low-maintenance power. Extra props should be carried on board to avoid weeks of layover time waiting for a new one in the event of damage. A lead line—as well as a depth finder—is also essential equipment since virtually the entire waterway runs through shoal water and is prone to silting.

Any waterway cruiser should be equipped with fender boards, long dock lines and spring lines for making fast to commercial piers, and heavy ground tackle—including a spare anchor—so the boatman can moor for the night out of a fairway with no danger of dragging back into the mainstream. Binoculars are useful for spotting marks. Close-mesh screens and mosquito netting are a must from June to August. And a single-side-band receiver will pick up 7268 kHz and 14.278 kHz on the waterway's informal, ham-operated radio network, which broadcasts the weather and other important cruising information.

Wildlife

The waterway coincides for almost its entire length with the Atlantic flyway, one of North America's main routes for migratory waterfowl. Every spring and fall, birds by the tens of thousands fly over the heads of cruising boatmen. The species include Canada geese, snow geese, mallards, canvasbacks, buffleheads, scaup, coots and teal. In numerous places down the coast, wildlife refuges have been set aside as way stations for the migrants. The Assateague Island refuge, in Maryland, also boasts tiny Japanese sika deer, as well as a herd of wild ponies whose progenitors are said to have been stranded there by shipwrecked Spanish galleons. Cape Romain Migratory Bird Refuge in South Carolina shelters numerous waterfowl including heron, pelicans and teal. And the Blackbeard Island, Georgia, refuge is the home of hundreds of alligators, among other things.

Sports

The mid-Atlantic region offers extremely fertile fishing grounds, ranging from fresh-water tributaries through brackish inner sounds and bays to the deep waters of the ocean. Chesapeake Bay has 202 varieties of fish—including striped bass, flounder, speckled trout and bluefish. It is also famous for its blue crabs and the hard-shell clams that can be reaped from its sand and mud flats. Along the ocean shores of North and South Carolina, inshore varieties such as bluefish, Spanish or king mackerel, and striped bass can be caught either by surf casting or from one of the area's many fishing piers. For offshore fishing, charter sport-fishing boats are available—especially along North Carolina's Outer Banks—for fully outfitted expeditions in search of marlin, sailfish and tuna. South Carolina's Waccamaw River is justly renowned for largemouth bass, bream and crappies. And the coastal rivers of Georgia just off the waterway are alive with pickerel, catfish, bluegill and sunfish.

No license is required for salt-water fishing in this region. Prices for fresh-water licenses for out-of-staters run from around $3.00 in Georgia to over $10.00 for a season in South Carolina.

The ocean fronts of North and South Carolina and the Georgia Sea Islands are trimmed with sand beaches; swimming is superb from June to September when the Atlantic surf reaches temperatures of up to 78°. The Chesapeake is also a good spot for swimming, except in July and August when sea nettles—a stinging jellyfish—swarm throughout the bay.

Regional Boating Regulations

Numbers 3 and 4 of the *Coast Pilots* each devote a chapter to local navigation regulations along the waterway. A considerable number of these rules apply only to commercial vessels; nonetheless, the *Coast Pilots* include regulations that pleasure boaters also must obey. The Intracoastal Waterway injunction against excessive speeding reads: "Vessels shall proceed at a speed which will not endanger other vessels or structures and will not interfere with any work in progress incident to maintaining, improving, surveying or marking the channel." Some waterway stretches have posted speed limits; others have "no wake" signs—warnings designed to reduce the destructive effect of wakes against channel banks, moored boats and docks.

Other regulations include those governing the use of locks like the two on the Dismal Swamp Canal. To inform the lockmaster of an intention to lock through, a boatman must sound his whistle two long and two short blasts before he gets within a quarter mile of the lock. The signal for opening a drawbridge is three long signals, given from a safe distance. Regulations also determine the hours, if any, that a drawbridge is inoperative.

Major Provisioning Ports

Hardly a spot exists along the mid-Atlantic coast where a full-service port with fuel, water, ice and food supplies—as well as medical and repair facilities—is not within a day's run. Nevertheless, a few ports make especially good stopovers:

> **Annapolis:** A natural stopover on the Maryland shore of Chesapeake Bay. The port's three harbors offer all provisioning and repair services, some by nationally known boatbuilders and sailmakers.
> **Norfolk:** Virginia's main port with facilities for all craft from day sailers to nuclear submarines. Numerous marinas and boatyards provide all needed services, including major engine repairs.
> **Morehead City:** In North Carolina, the home of a sizable sport-fishing fleet. The port is an important service center for yachts along the North Carolina coast, providing such rare benefits as hired divers who will go overboard to make underwater repairs.
> **Georgetown:** A major South Carolina port. Near the city's waterfront are marinas, electronic sales and service shops and an off-channel anchorage.

> **Charleston:** A prime cruising stop in South Carolina, even for vessels that do not require supplies or service. Three yacht-repair areas contain specialists in every important marine service.
> **Savannah:** Eight miles up the Savannah River in Georgia. Pleasure craft should remain in the marinas and yacht clubs near the mouth of the river at Thunderbolt and Isle of Hope, rather than running up to the commercial docks in the city.

Coast Guard Stations

The Coast Guard maintains stations with search-and-rescue facilities at: Still Pond, Baltimore, Annapolis, Taylors Island, Crisfield and Piney Point, Maryland; Dahlgren, Milford Haven, Cape Charles, Norfolk Station and Little Creek, Virginia; Elizabeth City, Oregon Inlet, Cape Hatteras, Hatteras Inlet, Ocracoke, Hobucken, Cape Lookout, Fort Macon, Swansboro, Wrightsville Beach and Oak Island, North Carolina; Charleston, South Carolina; Tybee Island and St. Simons Island, Georgia.

Charts and Publications

Proper charts for a cruise in the mid-Atlantic waterways can be selected from *Nautical Chart Catalog 1*, for the Atlantic and Gulf coasts, published by the National Ocean Survey *(address below)*. Also available from the National Ocean Survey and its sales agents are the following: tide tables and tidal current tables for the entire Atlantic coast; tidal current charts for upper Chesapeake Bay and Charleston Harbor; *United States Coast Pilots 3 and 4*; and Marine Weather Services Charts MSC-3 (Manasquan, New Jersey, to Cape Hatteras, North Carolina), MSC-4 (Cape Hatteras to Savannah, Georgia) and MSC-5 (Savannah to Apalachicola, Florida). Volumes I and II of the light lists specify the region's aids to navigation and can be obtained by writing to the Superintendent of Documents, Government Printing Office, Washington, D.C. The weekly *Notice to Mariners*—an update of *Coast Pilots*—is available from the Defense Mapping Agency:

> Defense Mapping Agency Depot
> 5801 Tabor Avenue
> Philadelphia, Pennsylvania 19120

> National Ocean Survey
> Distribution Division, C44
> 6501 Lafayette Avenue
> Riverdale, Maryland 20840

The following publications are of particular help to cruising boatmen of the mid-Atlantic waterways:

> Blanchard, Fessenden S., and William T. Stone, *A Cruising Guide to the Chesapeake.* New York: Dodd, Mead & Company.
> Matthews, William B., Jr., *Guide to Cruising Maryland Waters.* Andover, Massachusetts: National Book Corporation.
> Roscoe, Robert S., and Fessenden S. Blanchard, *A Cruising Guide to the Southern Coast.* New York: Dodd, Mead & Company.
> *Tidewater Virginia Boating Guide.* Washington, D.C.: Williams & Heintz Map Corp.
> *Waterway Guide, Mid-Atlantic Edition.* Annapolis, Maryland: Marine Annuals, Inc.

Two small cruising sloops slide beneath a span of the Chesapeake Bay Bridge, which crosses the bay at its three-and-a-half-mile waist between the Annapolis shore and Kent Island—at the heart of the Chesapeake's best cruising area.

Two Chesapeake watermen transfer their catch of blue crabs from wire crab pots to bushel baskets ready for market. The bay's mix of fresh and salt water is ideal for producing this prized crustacean, which spawns near the mouth and moves up the bay to feed. Crabs are trapped and sold everywhere on the bay. Bay sailors relish them steamed with a peppery sauce and washed down with plenty of ice-cold beer.

Typical of the lush, inviting Chesapeake coastline is this stretch of the eastern shore near the mouth of the Tred Avon River. Here the estuary's bank reaches in between tree-lined estates and farmlands, providing placid coves perfect for overnight anchorage. In the distance the Tred Avon takes a sweeping right-hand curve into the 17th Century town of Oxford—which today offers a yacht club, a dockside restaurant, a marina and four boatyards.

Chesapeake Bay

Chesapeake Bay, which thrusts nearly 200 miles into Maryland and Virginia, is bordered by an astonishing 5,000 miles of filigreed shoreline. It was created a mere 10,000 years ago by the outflowing of the Susquehanna, the Potomac and some 40 other rivers that now empty their water —and silt—into it. Despite its size, the bay remains shallow, with an average depth of only 30 feet.

Nevertheless, the Chesapeake is one of the most intensely used bays on the American coast. More than 200,000 pleasure-boaters sail out of home ports in the bay, and each year thousands more visit the bay to cruise or to use it as a route to and from the waterway sections to the south. In addition, some 8,000 commercial fishermen—still known by the old English name of watermen—haul in some 430 million pounds of fish and 85 million pounds of oysters and crabs from the remarkably fertile waters. Scarcely one of these small craft has avoided the endemic hazard of sailing these waters: running aground. But the soft sand and mud bottom makes grounding more an inconvenience than a danger; tides are modest, and the mariner can usually slide free with a tug on his anchor or a thrust of his engine.

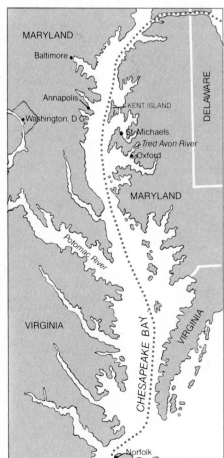

CHESAPEAKE BAY: THE EASTERN SHORE

St. Michaels, a small, pre-Revolutionary
town on boat-thronged Miles River, offers fine
waterfront restaurants, full-service marinas
and docking facilities—and the Chesapeake
Bay Maritime Museum, headquartered
in these three 19th Century houses. Outdoor
exhibits include an old Chesapeake Bay
lighthouse, a fleet of indigenous small craft
and the topmast oyster sloop J. T. Leonard,
built in 1882 and shown here at dockside.

Turn-of-the-century Chesapeake Bay skipjacks
are still used by a number of the bay's
watermen to dredge for oysters. Although the
crew does its actual dredging under sail, all
skipjacks carry a rudderless, motor-driven
craft, called a push boat, on davits. At the end
of the day, the push boat is unshipped and
rigged astern so that it can literally push the
oystermen home with their catch.

As two of its nine-man crew position their weight far to windward on
hiking boards, a 33-foot sailing log canoe reaches smartly along in the
annual Fourth of July race. This double-ended craft—unique to
the Chesapeake—evolved from an Indian dugout design that, with the
addition of a sailing rig, served early English settlers as a work boat.
The canoe was adapted for racing in the late 1800s, by which time it
had acquired outriggers, a centerboard and oversized sails.

On quiet Edenton Bay in upper Albemarle Sound sits the Penelope Barker House, a double-galleried, pre-Revolutionary house where the Edenton Tea Party of 1774—a boycott of British goods—was organized by a number of the town's patriotic women. Adjacent to the Barker House is Edenton's public dock, where visiting boats can lay over in water depths of at least 10 feet. Edenton's only marina, a half mile up Pembroke Creek in the northwest corner of the bay, is not accessible to boats that draw more than four feet.

Towering a majestic 208 feet above the water on Hatteras Island's elbow, Cape Hatteras Light warns boatmen of the area's treacherous shoals, justly named the "Graveyard of the Atlantic" for the more than 600 ships they have claimed. Southeast of the lighthouse, on the Pamlico Sound side of the island, is the village of Hatteras, the only port with cruising facilities on Hatteras Island. The home of a large charter sport-fishing fleet, many of Hatteras' docks are brusquely commercial, with only a few spaces for transients. Accommodations for cruising yachtsmen can also be found at the neighboring Outer Banks ports of Ocracoke, Manteo and Wanchese.

In the waters off Cape Hatteras, three surf casters play their lines and wait for a strike. Here the wide, warm, upward-flowing Gulf Stream meets southward-flowing currents of colder northern waters to produce superb grounds for both inshore and offshore fishing. Sea trout, striped bass, bluefish, and Spanish and king mackerel all can be caught from the beach or off one of the Banks' eight ocean piers. For deep-sea game fish such as marlin, sailfish, dolphin and tuna, charter sport-fishing boats with captains are available in such sound-side harbors as Hatteras, Oregon Inlet and Ocracoke.

Banks and Sounds

After the Intracoastal Waterway emerges from the Dismal Swamp Canal to thread its way down the North Carolina coast, running through peninsulas and across stretches of open water, it passes in the lee of a thin strip of barrier islands called the Outer Banks. This 150-mile string of sea-forged dunes and ridges forms a natural dike between the turbulent Atlantic and the brackish Carolina sounds: Currituck, Albemarle, Pamlico, Roanoke, Croatan and Core. Wide for the most part (Pamlico Sound is up to 25 miles across) and shallow (average depth 10 to 20 feet), the sounds can be whipped into a nasty chop by the wind. And their ever-shifting shoals can make piloting hazardous.

Nevertheless, to an adventurous boatman the sounds are worth crossing. Along the Banks are miles of ocean beach, giant dunes, uncluttered vistas and superb sport fishing. On Roanoke Island, the New World's first English-speaking colonists came ashore; in a small harbor on Ocracoke Island, the infamous Blackbeard was cornered and beheaded. And the wildness of those early times still lives—in the clashing seas and whistling winds.

Pleasure-boaters who are in search of more placid scenes have another option along the Carolina waterway. They can head inland up the labyrinth of estuaries to visit quiet creeks and coves. Here are out-of-the-way towns such as Edenton, Bath and New Bern, all once-prosperous 18th Century seaports and still very much alive as lovely places to visit.

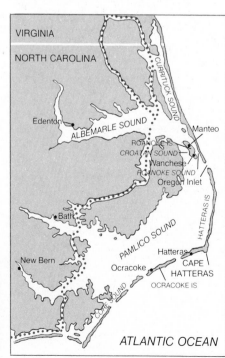

Carolina Channels

Along half its length from Norfolk to the Florida border, the Intracoastal Waterway passes through long, straight land cuts and narrow rivers. Nowhere is this canal-like aspect of the waterway more evident than in the 65-mile stretch shown here, along the coast of South Carolina.

Just south of the popular deep-sea fishing town of Little River, the waterway enters the Pine Island Cut, a 26-mile-long canal that slices through high-banked, heavily wooded countryside. It then feeds into the Waccamaw River, one of the most beautiful stretches in the entire system. Here the boatman slides through abandoned rice fields and lush, moss-hung cypress swamps for some 28 miles until reaching Georgetown. A major seaport with three marinas and two boat-repair facilities, Georgetown is noted for two culinary specialties: smoked sturgeon —caught in the Waccamaw River—and caviar. Below Georgetown, the waterway crosses Winyah Bay and continues into another land cut.

The cruising along these watery thoroughfares is totally protected and generally peaceful—though traffic may be heavy during the peak migratory seasons for pleasure boats in fall and spring. Despite the Corps of Engineers' effort to maintain a constant 12-foot depth, the sides of channels constantly fill with silt. Thus, skippers should pay close attention to channel markers, with their distinctive yellow Intracoastal Waterway markings. Furthermore, this single, short stretch has three of the low-clearance highway and railroad drawbridges that are a constant cruising hazard all along the waterway. The appropriate *Coast Pilot* should be kept close at hand and consulted for the times of day these bridges operate, and for any special regulations or procedures involved in passing through them.

A highway swing span in the Pine Island Cut two and a half miles south of Little River swivels open to permit the passage of the craft from which this picture was taken. When approaching a drawbridge, the skipper should give three blasts of a horn or whistle to alert the bridge operator; and he should give the warning while there is still time to stop in case land traffic holds the span momentarily closed.

Under early morning November skies, a Florida-bound snowbird—a nickname given to the thousands of boats that flock south along the Intracoastal Waterway in the fall—cuts through still waters in the lower reaches of the Waccamaw River. During the peak season, traffic on the Pine Island Cut/Waccamaw River passage frequently tops 100 boats a day as cruisers, small outboards, tugs, barges and commercial fishing boats compete for space in the constricted waterways.

Two Carolinians in a small outboard fish for bream and other pan fish close to the heavily wooded banks of Longwood Island in the Waccamaw River. In this and similar sections of The Ditch, where the forest crowds right up to the channel's edge, the trees are often undermined and toppled by wakes from passing boats, presenting a serious navigational hazard. To reduce the chance of colliding with a fallen tree trunk—and to cut down on damage to the banks—boatmen should proceed slowly and create as little wake as possible.

Charleston's downtown waterfront boulevard, South Battery, is lined with the gracious antebellum mansions and golden palmettos typical of the city's well-preserved residential area. Houses of the period were built with one to three pillared galleries on their south sides in order to catch the southerly summer breezes. The galleries were also gathering places where gentlefolk sipped mint juleps, discussed the rice and cotton crops, and—at half past four in the morning on April 12, 1861—watched the Confederate attack on Fort Sumter.

Charles Towne Landing, northwest of downtown Charleston, holds 100 acres of lush, formal gardens and lagoons like the one shown here —all part of a historical reconstruction of the city's original settlement in 1670. Though Charles Towne Landing is on the Ashley River, there are no public docking facilities. Yachtsmen wanting to visit here or the area's other restored gardens—Middleton Place, Magnolia and Cypress—should plan to do so by rented car.

Fort Sumter at the mouth of Charleston Harbor is now a national monument with no pleasure-boat docks; but it is accessible to history buffs via tour boats from the mainland. The pentagonal fort perches on a partially submerged sandspit just northwest of Charleston's 35-foot-deep entrance channel. The channel is protected on both sides by mile-and-a-half-long jetties, making the access to Charleston Harbor from the sea one of the quietest approaches to a major city anywhere on the Atlantic coast.

Charleston

South Carolina's second largest city and major seaport, Charleston, is probably the best harbor of refuge on the southern Atlantic coast—and has been for centuries. As early as the 1770s, Charleston was a thriving and prosperous seaport; at times more than 350 ships rode at anchor in its naturally protected harbor.

There are several entrances to this harbor: through the main sea channel seven miles southeast of the city, or from either of the Intracoastal Waterway channels on the east and west sides of the harbor. When approaching Charleston either way from the waterway, the boatman should carefully check the bridge regulations in the current *Coast Pilot,* since the drawbridges on both channels open only at certain restricted hours.

Once inside the harbor, a series of ranges guide boats to the municipal marina on the Ashley River. The marina has 20 slips for transient boats and 283 spaces for local boats, many of which lie along floating docks designed to allow for Charleston's six-foot tidal range.

From the centrally located marina the boatman can easily make an exploratory tour on foot or bicycle to enjoy Charleston's narrow streets, 18th and 19th century houses, gardens, intricate wrought-iron gates and historic buildings. The Dock Street Theatre, built in 1736 and one of the oldest playhouses in the country, is a particular favorite of visitors. Also famous are Charleston's restaurants, known all up and down the Intracoastal Waterway for such regional specialties as she-crab soup, beaten biscuits and buttermilk ice cream.

The vine-covered ruin of an antebellum slave hospital, part of the
cotton-growing empire of Retreat Plantation, still stands on the
southern tip of St. Simons Island. This land is now part of the Sea
Island Golf Club, one of several resort facilities in the area. Northeast
of the club and fronting on the Intracoastal Waterway is partially
restored Fort Frederica, built in 1736 by Georgia's founder, James
Oglethorpe, and the site in 1742 of the colony's successful repulse of
an invasion by the Spanish. Pleasure-boaters visiting St. Simons
can find a full-service marina on Lanier Island, south of the lift bridge
that crosses the Intracoastal Waterway to link the islands.

The 27-room Crane Cottage, on Jekyll Island, is one of 11 remaining
tycoons' mansions that once belonged to the families of the exclusive
Jekyll Island Club. The members of the club—including Goulds,
Rockefellers, Vanderbilts, Astors and Morgans—took their meals in a
communal clubhouse, allowed visitors to stay no longer than two
weeks and referred to all their guests as "strangers." In 1947, sixty-one
years after its founding, the once-sacrosanct retreat was sold to the
state of Georgia. The island is now a state park, and the complex of
millionaires' houses in the old village—which can be seen from the
waterway—is within easy walking distance of the Jekyll Island Marina.

Georgia Sea Islands

From the Savannah River, the Intracoastal Waterway threads its way for 140 miles behind Georgia's islands—Wassaw, Ossabaw, St. Catherines, Blackbeard, Sapelo, St. Simons, Sea Island, Jekyll and Cumberland. Unlike the Outer Banks of the Carolinas, these islands lie close to the mainland and are separated from it by sinuous rivers. Most of the islands are wide, fertile and forested, with fine white sand beaches fronting the ocean and broad marshes on their inner shores.

This rich intermingling of land and water breeds an astonishing profusion of wildlife. For centuries the islands were the hunting grounds of the Guale Indians, who stalked waterfowl, raccoon, wild turkey, bear and deer. A succession of colonizers moved in to claim the area's riches—Spanish, English, and an American plantation aristocracy of rice and cotton growers. In the late 1800s, the lands were turned back into hunting grounds—the private retreats of wealthy industrialists. Today, only three islands maintain some of the aura of genteel privilege—clubby Sea Island and St. Simons, and the somewhat more frenetic Jekyll. The rest are slowly returning to a state of nature, mostly as state and federal wildlife areas.

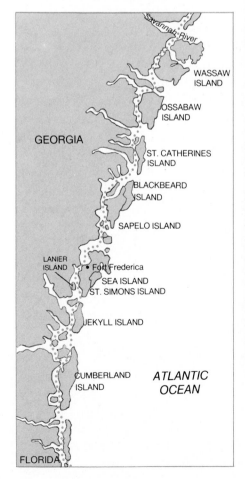

Two wild horses—probably descendants of a plantation-era herd —graze in the salt marshes of Cumberland Island. Southernmost of Georgia's Sea Islands, Cumberland has been largely taken over by the U.S. Park Service, which preserves its 32,400-acre holdings as undeveloped national seashore. Visitors can anchor their boats along the riverbank on the western shore of the island.

7 It was a June midafternoon on the Laguna Madre, the 120-mile salt-water corridor that lies between Corpus Christi and Port Brownsville, Texas, on the Gulf Intracoastal Waterway. The southeast wind, blowing hot and steady at 15 knots, flapped the canvas top of our 38-foot powerboat, *Final Edition,* as my wife Peggy and I chugged along at a leisurely eight knots. Well off to port we could see Padre Island, its white dunes seeming to dance above the water as heat waves rose from them. Close by to starboard, stretching to the horizon, lay the great expanse of the King Ranch—a million-acre cattle empire founded a century ago by a shrewd old steamboat captain named Richard King. At my

FLORIDA AND THE GULF

side I noticed that Peggy was intently focusing her binoculars on something to starboard. I squinted toward the King Ranch mud flat and asked, "What's a dog doing out there?" Peggy did not immediately reply. Then she handed me the binoculars and said, "Look at the droopy tail, the pointed ears." It was a coyote—the first of six we were to see while cruising the big lagoon. It trotted across the hard-packed mud to the water's edge, tested the water tentatively with its paw, then eased in a few inches, apparently ready to fish. As we drew close, it saw us, turned, gave us a slow over-the-shoulder look and retreated.

No great adventure, but part of the lure of powering down the Gulf Intracoastal Waterway. Where else, from the deck of a boat, could you watch a coyote forage his meal? For Peggy and me, such an incident is the very stuff of cruising—seeing the unexpected, the unusual, and doing it at a lazy pace.

Peggy and I have put in more than two decades and many thousands of miles of cruising together. Since 1952, when as a baseball reporter I came down to Florida to cover spring training for a Boston radio station—and stayed for life—we have lived in and around the Tampa Bay area. We have cruised both sides of the Florida peninsula: the east coast with its high-rise condominiums and lunar launch pads, and the west coast with its unpretentious fishing villages thinly populated with salty Florida-cracker natives. And we have poked endlessly around the bleached Keys with their legends of 18th Century pirates. But to our special tastes, no cruising ground can quite match the one that passes right through our own backyard: the southern portion of the great inland waterway system, beginning with the Florida section of the Atlantic Intracoastal Waterway, and continuing westward along the Gulf Intracoastal Waterway.

The segment of waterway that offers us the strongest sense of discovery and surprise is the section of the Gulf waterway that starts at the Florida panhandle, some 150 miles north of Tampa. Here is a wondrous combination of natural beauty and human engineering—a string of inlets, sounds, bays, rivers and lakes connected by man-made canals. On it a yachtsman can travel 1,059 continuous miles all the way to the Mexican border. The Gulf Intracoastal Waterway was originally designed and built for commercial purposes. But for the inquisitive boatman who is willing to thread a path through the trawlers and barges, and wait his turn at the half-dozen locks along the way, the waterway offers a matchless string of fascinating contrasts.

When Peggy and I leave our home port of St. Petersburg to make the trip west, one of the first stretches we must negotiate is the so-called Lonesome Leg. This is the run from the Anclote Keys to Carrabelle, a distance run of 150 to 180 miles (depending on which course you chart) across the northeast corner of the Gulf. The Lonesome Leg is well named; it runs through open water, and there are no easy stops when the waters get rough—which they frequently do. Until 1974 there weren't even any markers on the route, and I take a certain personal pride in the knowledge that now there are. As a newspaperman

Bahia Mar Marina on Florida's Gold Coast—a 100-mile strip of luxury docks and apartments lining the Atlantic waterway—has everything from marine railways to baby-sitter service.

Outdoors Editor for the St. Petersburg Times for 20 years, Red Marston has cruised some 22,000 miles from Maine to Texas—mostly through Florida and Gulf Coast waters.

and a boatman, I occasionally covered the rescue of lost strangers from up north. After two disastrous episodes in which six lives were lost, I helped persuade the Coast Guard to put up half a dozen lighted buoys. Strangers still get lost out there, but when they call for help, at least now they can give their positions to guide the rescuers.

At the end of the Lonesome Leg lies Apalachicola. Here the waterway goes inland and turns west, wending among tall pines and alongside steep embankments, then crossing wooded lakes that look more northern than southern. Peggy and I have a warm feeling for Apalachicola; a friendly policeman there once took Peggy grocery shopping in his patrol car when we came ashore in need of supplies, and an obliging postman opened up the post office after hours just to let us pick up some accumulated mail.

Usually we prefer to skim quickly past the Alabama coast, with its mélange of shrimp-trawl ports and busy shipyards. But then we like to linger a little in Mississippi, with its gracious waterfront mansions, some of which have been turned into elegant restaurants. I remember on one recent cruise sitting in the high-ceilinged dining room of a French restaurant in Biloxi, overlooking Mississippi Sound, while the chef served up an extraordinary dish of mushrooms stuffed with fresh crab meat. For us, Mississippi also brings to mind a genial commodore of the Gulfport Yacht Club; he once took us crab fishing and then served up a magnificent crab gumbo made from the catch.

Past Mississippi and into Louisiana, and there we feel the real impact of heavy industry along the waterway. Tugboats, push boats, barges and trawlers cram the channels, and more than once I have been startled to see a seaplane appear out of nowhere and skim to a landing in a tiny space between our own boat and the ponderous vessel beside us.

To get past New Orleans we lock through the city's canals—an intimidating experience at first, partly because of the danger of grinding against the rough locksides in the turbulent water; partly because the traffic is so heavy, commercial vessels have priority, and a small pleasure boat may have a long wait. Nevertheless, at every point along the way, we found that the lockmasters will obligingly squeeze our small craft into the locks alongside one of their regular hefty customers. The bargemen themselves were equally amiable, always ready to throw us a line for a raft-up, and then to chat companionably while we all waited for the water to churn.

For all its busy industry, this Louisiana segment of the waterway also offers long unspoiled stretches—reedy marshes that extend as far as the eye can see and bayous shadowed in towering cypress trees. One night, after hours of steering a course among mammoth oil barges, we eased *Final Edition* into a little creek off Lake Cocodrie, 15 miles east of busy Morgan City—and virtually had to nudge an alligator out of the way to anchor. Then, while we slept, bullfrogs croaked all night.

The place with the most startling contrasts of all is Texas, whose coast is splotched with nodding oil pumps, chemical plants and freight docks; in between is pure open wilderness. For example, the Laguna Madre, where we saw the coyotes, is a giant shallow estuary that teems with wildlife. Thousands of waterfowl seek shelter there, especially during the winter. A single raft of ducks may stretch out for miles. Cormorants jostle one another for space on the sand bars. Immaculate white pelicans fly in formation through the blue sky, looking as if they were freshly laundered and drying out in the pure winds aloft. On one trip Peggy and I even saw a reddish egret lurching about, first in one direction, then in another, and, unlike the shy coyote, seeming to clown for its audience. This playful bird, in fact, has remained for us a kind of symbol of the waterway's surprises. Almost extinct in the early part of this century, the reddish egret is making a comeback in a rookery protected by the Audubon Society—just down the coast from Galveston's supertanker berths, teeming Port Arthur and Houston's space center.

by Red Marston

A platoon of white pelicans perches on a sand bar in the Ten Thousand Islands, an enormous cluster of sandspits and mangrove colonies on Florida's Gulf Coast just north of the Everglades. Water depths in among the islands are too shallow for most cruising boats, but a visitor can anchor at a channel edge and explore by dinghy. Besides good bird watching (herons, egrets, ibis, cormorants) he will find some excellent fishing for snook, redfish and tarpon.

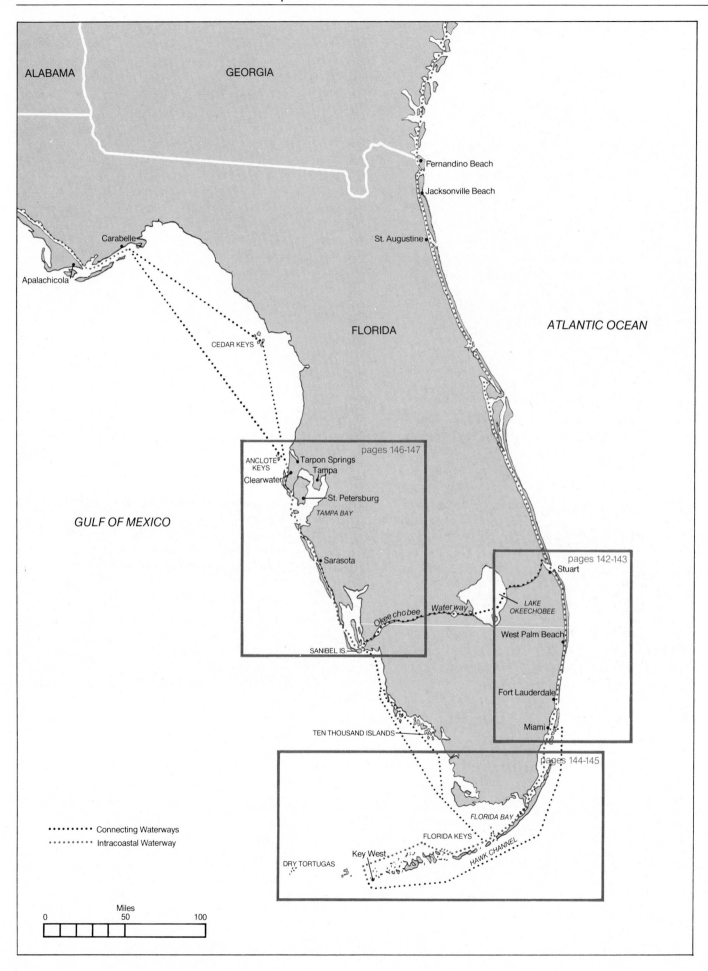

ALABAMA

GEORGIA

Fernandino Beach

Jacksonville Beach

St. Augustine

Carabelle

Apalachicola

FLORIDA

ATLANTIC OCEAN

CEDAR KEYS

pages 146-147

ANCLOTE KEYS

Tarpon Springs

Tampa

Clearwater

St. Petersburg

TAMPA BAY

GULF OF MEXICO

Sarasota

pages 142-143

Stuart

LAKE OKEECHOBEE

Okee cho bee   Waterway

West Palm Beach

SANIBEL IS.

Fort Lauderdale

Miami

TEN THOUSAND ISLANDS

pages 144-145

FLORIDA BAY

FLORIDA KEYS

•••••• Connecting Waterways

······ Intracoastal Waterway

DRY TORTUGAS   Key West

HAWK CHANNEL

Miles

0   50   100

A Sweep of Sun Coast

The subtropical coastal belt of the Southern United States, stretching across five states and 2,000 miles from Fernandina Beach, Florida, on the Atlantic to Brownsville, Texas, on the Gulf of Mexico, has tantalized sailors for more than four centuries. When Spanish explorer Juan Ponce de Leon set foot on American soil in 1513, near the site of St. Augustine, he named the place Florida—isle of flowers—believing the region to be separate from the mainland. In search of gold and rejuvenating waters, he cruised southward to the Keys. En route he poked into many of the sheltered lagoons that form present-day Florida's resort-crammed, East Coast portion of the Intracoastal Waterway.

On the west side of the peninsula, the Gulf Coast starts a great curve that sweeps upward to the Florida panhandle, and then west *(below)* to the Rio Grande. Except for a few connecting legs—indicated by black dotted lines—the curve is traversed by segments of the Intracoastal Waterway *(blue dotted lines)*. Along this curve the boatman encounters a jumble of barrier islands and inlets on Florida's west coast, then the river-laced bayous of Louisiana, and finally the majestic processional of Texas' Laguna Madre.

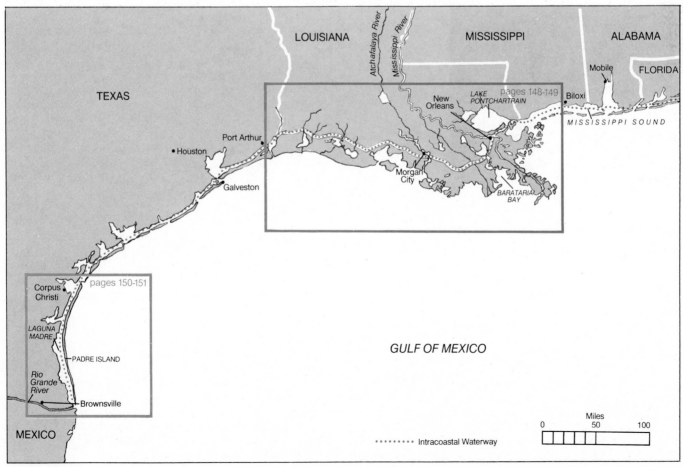

Winds and Weather

The Florida and Gulf Coast region is dominated by a humid sub-tropical climate with hot, wet summers and mild, clear winters. Though conditions vary locally, the best cruising weather is from October through May, when the sun shines almost every day, and average temperatures range from a comfortable 54° to 74° at New Orleans, on the region's northern fringe, and from 69° to 79° at southernmost Key West. Winter also brings a sharp drop in rainfall, but the boatman must be prepared nevertheless for an almost daily ritual of brief showers. And in the Florida Gulf, he must also occasionally cope with winter northers that come whipping down at 20 to 50 knots, sending temperatures plummeting and yachtsmen to shelter for two to four days at a time. Heavy fogs are rare, and the light ground fogs that form in such areas as Tampa Bay and the Louisiana bayous rarely survive the heat of the morning sun.

Breezes are bountiful all year; typically, the winds rise from the east and southeast, gradually shifting to southwest off Florida's west coast, and reach seven to 12 knots each afternoon before dying down after sunset. Off the Texas coast, however, winds blow at an average of 12 knots well into the night.

The region's notoriously destructive hurricanes—tropical cyclones with winds in excess of 63 knots—occur only sporadically, and almost never during the winter months. Although there are dozens of storms during the June-to-October hurricane season, only about five achieve hurricane force each year. These are closely tracked and their positions constantly reported so that boats have ample time to find a hurricane hole.

Tides and Currents

The tides on the Gulf range from a barely perceptible few inches to a modest four feet. Nor are they much more impressive on Florida's Atlantic coast, where the tidal range drops from a maximum of about six feet at Fernandina Beach in the north to about three feet in Biscayne Bay—with tides near zero at Cape Canaveral in mid-peninsula. So weak are the tides on Florida's west coast that stiff north winds actually stop them from coming in.

Tidal currents are generally sluggish, seldom exceeding a knot or two, but they can be tricky at entrances to narrow inlets and passages. For example, the negligible tidal current in Florida's east-coast waterway rises to seven knots at St. Lucie Inlet. By contrast, in some segments of the Louisiana bayous, weak tidal currents are often overwhelmed by strong fresh-water currents from lakes and rivers, especially after heavy rainfall.

Pilotage

For boatmen who stick to the well-marked waterways, the region's basically placid waters offer no piloting problems. But just beyond the dredged channels are shallows, subject to shoaling, whose charted depths are unreliable. A depth recorder is vital, though in many areas, such as Florida Bay, skippers can estimate depth by reading the water's color: black, brown or white water, reflecting coral or sand near the surface, can be no more than a foot deep; blue or green water ranges up to nine feet.

While shallow coastal water is endemic to the entire region, other hazards are peculiar to specific areas. On Florida's east coast, frequent stops for closed drawbridges combine with stringent speed regulations to make waterway cruising slow. But sailors who opt for a faster offshore run must contend with tricky currents and shifting shoals when entering or leaving the waterway. Yachtsmen should be alert for floats marking submerged

lobster and stone-crab pots in the Keys, and for oil rigs and submerged pipes as far as 70 miles offshore along the Louisiana and Texas coasts. In the bayous, floating masses of hyacinths infest many streams.

Boats and Special Equipment

The shallowness of the region's waters outside the dredged channels makes it advisable to cruise in boats drawing less than four feet. Vessels requiring five feet or more should plan on a lot of offshore running. Whatever boat is used should have its cockpit covered with a canvas top as protection against intense sun.

Small, light anchors are useful in the powdery bottom sand found in many parts of the region. Be sure to bring a dinghy for exploring waters barely knee-deep. A VHF radio is essential in places like the Louisiana bayous, where local boatmen use it instead of a whistle for signaling lockmasters and one another.

Cruising supplies should include suntan lotion and insect repellent. And the skipper who plans to pilot by reading the water should have sunglasses with gray or tan lenses. Those with green, blue or yellow tints can provide misleading depth clues.

Wildlife

The shores of the Southern waterways provide the ideal habitat for an enormous variety of resident and migratory wildlife. Two of the smaller Florida Keys, Howe and Big Pine, are a refuge for the Key deer, a relative of the Southern whitetail. Farther west, on Bush Key in the Dry Tortugas, is the only North American nesting ground of the sooty tern, and in the summer the rookery is home to an estimated 100,000 adults. Although the National Park Service does not permit boatmen to land, they can watch the traffic jam through binoculars.

The Gulf Intracoastal Waterway affords prime opportunities for wildlife viewing. Sanibel Island, on Florida's Gulf Coast, has a large National Wildlife Refuge for migratory birds, including varieties of herons, ibis, ospreys and pelicans. Sailors on the Louisiana portion of the waterway can visit Avery Island's bird sanctuary, a favored haunt of egrets, and the Sabine Wildlife Refuge, where alligators bask on the bayou banks. Just north of Corpus Christi, Texas, is the Aransas National Wildlife Refuge, winter home of the last surviving whooping cranes. Not many miles south, near the waterway's end, is Padre Island, where hundreds of bird species live and visit, and coyotes wander the beaches.

Sports

From Florida's east coast down through the Keys and across the Gulf to Texas, sport fishing is a year-round pastime, and the grounds are among the world's best. Flats fishermen go after bonefish and permit (great pompano); surf casters hook into bluefish and flounder; offshore anglers challenge grouper, snapper and amber jack. Most demanding are the big game species: sailfish, giant tarpon, blue marlin (Florida record: 666 pounds). For the less adventurous with an appetite for shellfish, there are conch, crawfish, crab and shrimp to catch.

In Florida no license is necessary for salt-water sport fishing; Louisiana and Texas both require licenses. Daily limits and minimum-length requirements are enforced in all areas. Licenses and information are obtainable at local sporting-goods stores, sheriffs' offices, and state fish and wildlife departments.

The balmy Southern climate makes it possible to enjoy a full array of other sports and recreation all year long. Swimming in the Gulf and the Atlantic Ocean is excellent, with water temperatures averaging 75°. Skin diving and scuba diving, spearfishing, shelling and beachcombing are first rate. Sanibel Island's shells draw collectors from all over the world. When diving or beachcombing, check local regulations about picking up souvenirs: at Padre Island, it is illegal to keep an old Spanish coin; Florida, where treasure hunting is serious business, requires a $15,000 license and collects 25 per cent of the bounty.

Regional Boating Regulations

On Florida's section of the Intracoastal Waterway, speed regulations are spelled out in signs that warn, "Slow Down—Minimum Wake" and "Idle Speed—No Wake." Be conservative: a local enforcer's definition of minimum wake may differ from yours. Florida also permits visiting boats up to 90 days of travel with an out-of-state registration; for longer periods the skipper should apply to the county tax collector for a Florida permit.

Gulf Intracoastal Waterway regulations and speed limits should be followed in Louisiana and Texas waters.

Major Provisioning Ports

The boatman will find ample to lavish docking, fuel and supply facilities along both of Florida's coastlines and in the Keys. But as he travels west from the Florida panhandle, provisioning ports are scarcer. Some of the principal ones, beginning on Florida's east coast and moving to Texas, appear below.

Fernandina Beach: First stop in Florida. The state Marine Welcome Station supplies literature, information and a computer service for booking marina space along the boatman's itinerary.

Jacksonville Beach: Close to the airport, a natural storage, layover and fitting-out port for Northern boatmen starting a Florida cruise. Good marinas offer all services and repairs, with specialists handling everything from electronics to refrigeration.

Fort Lauderdale: A boating-oriented city with big, luxurious marinas where the skipper can find marine-supply stores, boatyards, and sailmaking and dinghy-manufacturing facilities.

Miami: Jumping off point for the Bahamas and the Caribbean, with plentiful marinas providing everything in storage, repairs, supplies and services.

Key West: Southernmost city in the continental United States. Waterfront space may be scarce because of the Navy base and shrimp industry. But Stock Island, three miles from downtown, has docking facilities, yards, and marinas with laundromats, restaurants, marine supplies and repairs.

Sarasota: Focal point for the barrier-island resorts along this section of Florida's Gulf Coast, with facilities ranging from marinas to fishing camps.

St. Petersburg: On the peninsula west of Tampa Bay. The city provides a large marina and complete repair facilities, both the do-it-yourself yard variety and operations that haul 100-foot boats.

Panama City: The best-equipped yacht port north of Tampa/St. Petersburg. A key spot in the coast's extensive summer-resort district; full-service marinas, restaurants and shore accommodations.

Biloxi: A charming blend of old and new on Mississippi's resort coast, with all facilities and services located around its two harbors.

New Orleans: West End, a huge basin on the south shore of Lake Pontchartrain, provides boatyards, repair shops, supply stores and two yacht clubs.

Corpus Christi: The westernmost major provisioning port on the Texas coast, it has boating facilities concentrated in two areas: Ingleside Cove, northeast of the waterway; and downtown, with berthing accommodations for several hundred boats, and a variety of marine services and supplies.

Coast Guard Stations

The Coast Guard maintains seven stations on Florida's east coast, three in the Keys and seven on the Gulf Coast; four in Louisiana; and seven in Texas. All stations monitor distress frequencies 156.8 mHz (Channel 16 VHF-FM) and 2182 kHz. A large number of Coast Guard radio stations and public coast stations in the three states monitor Channel 16. In addition, there are Coast Guard rescue-coordination centers at Miami and New Orleans.

Charts and Publications

All the charts necessary for cruising the Southern waterways can be selected from *Nautical Chart Catalog 1,* for the Atlantic and Gulf coasts, published by the National Ocean Survey. Also available from NOS and its sales agents are the following: tide tables and tidal current tables for the Atlantic Coast (which includes the Gulf Coast); *United States Coast Pilots 4* and *5;* and Marine Weather Service Charts MSC-5 (Savannah, Georgia, to Apalachicola, Florida) and MSC-6 (Morgan City, Louisiana, to Brownsville, Texas). Volume II of the light lists describes the entire region's aids to navigation and is available from the Superintendent of Documents. The weekly *Notice to Mariners,* which updates the *Coast Pilots,* is published by the Defense Mapping Agency. Addresses for all three agencies appear below.

National Ocean Survey
Distribution Division, C44
6501 Lafayette Avenue
Riverdale, Maryland 20840

Superintendent of Documents
U.S. Government Printing Office
Washington, D.C. 20402

Defense Mapping Agency Depot
5801 Tabor Avenue
Philadelphia, Pennsylvania 19120

The following publications give specifics on entering Florida and Gulf Coast harbors, finding anchorages and choosing layovers.

Griswold, G. J. L., *Southern Yacht Club Cruising Guide.* New Orleans: Southern Yacht Club.

O'Reilly, John, *Boater's Guide to the Upper Florida Keys.* Coral Gables, Fla.: University of Miami Press.

Roscoe, Robert S., and Fessenden S. Blanchard, *A Cruising Guide to the Southern Coast.* New York: Dodd, Mead and Company.

Sites, George L., *Boater's Guide to Biscayne Bay.* Coral Gables, Fla.: University of Miami Press.

Waterway Guide, Southern Edition. Annapolis, Md.: Marine Annuals, Inc.

Miami Beach's Hotel Row, a narrow sandspit that includes the most luxurious of the resort's 360 hotels, dominates the southernmost nine miles of Gold Coast ocean front. Many of these hotels provide temporary dock space for guests and visitors along Indian Creek, the long inlet at the right separating Hotel Row from the rest of Miami. Yachtsmen tying up here are within a few hundred yards of a meal, a room ashore—or a front-row table at a hotel nightclub.

The Gold Coast

The 70° temperatures, sun-gilt beaches and flamboyant resorts that annually lure vacationers to Florida's Atlantic Coast also make this area the world's most popular winter cruising grounds. Its heart is the plush, 100-mile southern stretch known as the Gold Coast. In the February peak of the vacation season, the region's 8,000 transient mooring spaces are crowded with pleasure craft, many of them migrants from the north that have funneled down along the Intracoastal Waterway.

Much of the cruising takes place along the waterway itself, whose shores are lined with marinas. Alternately, the boatman can head out of one of eight inlets to the Gulf Stream with its open water and fine sport fishing. Many yachtsmen also make excursions inland along canals that fringe the waterway on the west. At St. Lucie River, at the northern end of the Gold Coast, a boatman can turn west 350 miles across Florida, with a stopover at Lake Okeechobee, renowned for its largemouth bass. Or he can head south down the waterway, past West Palm Beach to Fort Lauderdale, with its 165 miles of canals, its home fleet of 15,000 pleasure craft and some of the most luxurious marinas anywhere. Here he will find everything from drive-on docks to cabin maids.

Ten miles below Fort Lauderdale the yachtsman encounters a shoaling and sometimes uncertain channel in upper Biscayne Bay leading to Miami, southern terminus of the Gold Coast and a jump-off point for cruises to the Florida Keys and the Bahamas. Here, as along the entire Gold Coast, the boatmen should keep an eye out for tricky currents and shoals and for posted speed limits.

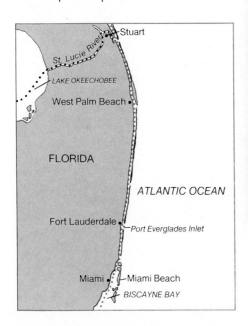

Two-way boat traffic moves as briskly as the posted speed limit (lower right) permits beneath the open arms of Fort Lauderdale's busy 17th Street Causeway Bridge. Like many of the other 41 bascule bridges that span the Gold Coast section of the Intracoastal Waterway and open on signal, this one limits its times of operation in deference to heavy automobile traffic; a digital clock (lower left) tells boatmen how long they must wait before the next opening can take place.

Outward bound for Port Everglades Inlet and a day of offshore fishing, a canopied cabin cruiser passes one of the many sumptuous estates built on filled land along the waterway in Fort Lauderdale. At far right is the entrance to one of the dozens of canals that web the city.

The Keys

The Florida Keys are so numerous that no map maker has ever claimed an accurate count of them all. Remnants of an ancient coral reef, they stretch invitingly over 150 miles between the resort centers of Miami and Key West, the southernmost spot in the continental United States. Named *cayos*—small islands—by 16th Century Spanish explorers, the Keys share the best of Florida's benign winter climate and the state's justly observed reputation for superb salt-water fishing. There are some 100 species of game in the waters around the Keys, including such heavyweight fighters as sailfish, marlin and bonito.

Cruising boats move through the Keys on two marked channels that parallel the island-hopping Overseas Highway. One of these, the stretch of Intracoastal Waterway that runs inside the Keys from Biscayne Bay into notoriously shoal Florida Bay, is suitable for shallow-draft boats only. Larger craft must take an outer route along Hawk Channel. This second passageway threads between the Keys and a long coral barrier reef some five miles to the east, and provides a fair degree of protection from Atlantic storms. From either channel, good harbors are available at Key Largo, Plantation Key, Upper Matecumbe Key, Vaca Key and Bahia Honda, the site of one of the finest beaches in the archipelago.

Beyond Bahia Honda, the two channels diverge; while the Hawk Channel continues southwest for another 42 miles directly to Key West, the inside route makes an abrupt dog-leg to the north. Boatmen following it are led into an 11-mile detour around the closely clustered lower keys, to reach Key West via Big Spanish Channel and the Gulf of Mexico. A third, more direct inner route that is indicated on some charts is not reliable and should not be used.

From Key West, yachtsmen with sturdy boats and adequate provisions can brave the choppy 75-mile trip across open water to the Dry Tortugas, to poke among the lonely islands and most particularly to explore the grim but fascinating bastion of Fort Jefferson *(opposite)*.

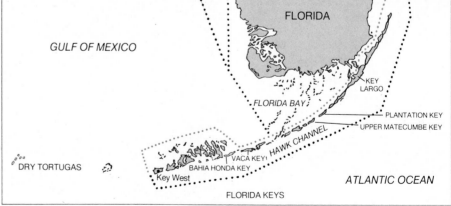

The arched spans of Seven-Mile Bridge carry a portion of the 158-mile Overseas Highway across open water between Knight Key and Bahia Honda Key. Like most bridges of the highway, which is an extension of the U.S. Route 1 from the Florida mainland to Key West, this one was originally a railroad bridge, put up in 1912 by real estate magnate Henry Flagler, who established Florida's first resort city at Palm Beach and then sought to extend his empire to Key West. The railroad was wrecked and abandoned after a destructive hurricane in 1935.

A school of striped porkfish swims along the bottom of an underwater state park off Key Largo, one of Florida's prime locales for snorkeling and scuba diving. In addition to more than 600 species of tropical reef fish, the park contains 40 varieties of living coral, which divers are permitted to explore and photograph—but never remove.

The eight-foot-thick walls of Fort Jefferson rise from a protective moat on Garden Key in the Dry Tortugas. Begun in 1846, it was designed to be the nation's largest coastal fort—a 16-acre brick hexagon bristling with 450 guns and manned by 1,500 artillerymen. Almost completed by the outbreak of the Civil War—when it was converted into a military prison—Fort Jefferson was declared obsolete and abandoned in 1874.

*Framed by a gnarled mangrove, a shallow-draft auxiliary rests off
Point Ybel, near the eastern tip of Sanibel. Like most of the barrier
islands along the Gulf Coast of Florida, Sanibel is almost completely
surrounded by sand flats; only boats that draw four feet or less
can safely enter the island's best harbor at Tarpon Bay.*

The Western Waterway

A combination of quiet sun-warmed waters and low-keyed opulence has made Florida's Gulf Coast increasingly attractive to pleasure cruisers. The area's most popular portion stretches from the sandy beaches of San Carlos Bay—the western end of the cross-Florida Okeechobee Waterway—150 miles north to the quaint sponge-fishing port of Tarpon Springs. Positioned along the coast at Clearwater, at St. Petersburg on Tampa Bay and at Sarasota to the south are superb marinas backed by first-class resorts, where many houses nestle among the bougainvillea and palmettos.

In between, the Intracoastal Waterway zigzags through wonderfully solitary bays and sounds, many of them so shallow that stiff north winds sometimes expose their sandy bottoms. To seaward of the waterway lies a chain of barrier islands, some of which have hardly changed since the days in the early 1800s when the Spanish pirate José Gaspar prowled these waters. One island still bears his nickname, Gasparilla. Today it is a favorite destination for fishermen pursuing the tarpon, redfish and snook that abound in adjacent Pine Island Sound.

At the southern edge of Pine Island Sound is crescent-shaped Sanibel, which has a fine beach and some of the world's best shell collecting; some specimens have been carried by currents from as far away as Mexico's Yucatán Peninsula.

Perhaps Sanibel's greatest attraction is the 11,000-acre National Wildlife Refuge, established in 1945 at the urging of the famed cartoonist and conservationist J. N. "Ding" Darling. Some 300 species of migratory birds have been spotted here at various times, including the great blue heron, the rarer wood ibis and the conspicuous roseate spoonbill.

A female anhinga, or water turkey, spreads its wings to dry in the sun while resting atop a mangrove in Sanibel's Ding Darling Wildlife Refuge. A particular curiosity among the dozens of waterfowl that visit the refuge, the anhinga swims with only its long neck and head out of the water. Because it lacks oil glands to keep its feathers dry, the anhinga performs its sunbathing ritual after every dip.

Shells lie ankle-deep on a beach along Sanibel's Gulf shore, which has yielded some 400 different species. So important a pastime is shell collecting on Sanibel that the island's main street is named Periwinkle Way, in honor of the small shell-bearing snail.

A bayou shrimp boat, folded nets strung from its rigging, chugs down placid Bayou Lafourche, a major route between the Intracoastal Waterway and the Gulf of Mexico. This vessel and the other shrimper behind it have the distinctive flaring bows and shallow hulls adapted from skiffs used by French pirate Jean Lafitte, who operated out of Barataria Bay almost two centuries ago. There are more than 1,000 such craft in the bayous, many owned and manned by Cajun families.

A row of bald cypresses, the most common of the wetland trees that thrive along the banks of bayous, cast their reflections on the still surface during a morning fog along the Intracoastal Waterway west of Morgan City. Fog and rain are regular occurrences in this subtropical region, especially in the winter months when the warm, moist winds off the Gulf of Mexico produce rain showers on 55 per cent of the days, providing much of the region's annual 60 inches.

A pair of tin-roofed trappers' shacks rest on pilings in a shallow off the Intracoastal Waterway near Lake Charles. Many of the region's 2,000 fur trappers spend their winters in the marshlands, where they collect about three million nutria and muskrat pelts during the December-to-February trapping season.

The Bayous

The 264-mile stretch of Gulf Intracoastal Waterway that traverses Louisiana's bayou country between New Orleans and Texas is fringed with a maze of interconnected rivers, creeks, lakes and canals where a boatman can happily lose himself for days on end. But he should be well provisioned before setting out; except for Lake Pontchartrain, New Orleans' main yachting center, there are no resort towns and barely a half-dozen marinas in the area. Furthermore, when moving in the waterway's main channel, he must be ready to contend with a steady parade of tugs, barges, shrimpers and workboats.

Almost anywhere along this busy thoroughfare, however, a turn of the wheel will put him in the brooding beauty of a misty backwater lined with majestic cypresses draped in gauzy Spanish moss. And few people possess the charm and hospitality of the French-speaking Cajuns who have fished and hunted here for more than two centuries, ever since their forebears came to French Louisiana in the late-18th Century, after being ousted from Nova Scotia by the English during the French and Indian War.

Many bayou-bound boatmen stop over in the convivial ambience of 35-mile-long Lake Pontchartrain, with its plentiful marinas and yacht clubs—all a short sail from New Orleans and its lively Latin Quarter.

West of New Orleans along the waterway, beyond the delta of the muddy Atchafalaya (pronounced chaffa-lye) River below Morgan City, begin the best opportunities for casual cruising. There are fine wilderness anchorages all the way to the Texas border. Bayou Lacassine, for example, offers an isolated stopover within a wildlife refuge that teems each winter with some of the half-million blue and snow geese that fly in from their homes in northern Canada, 3,000 miles away.

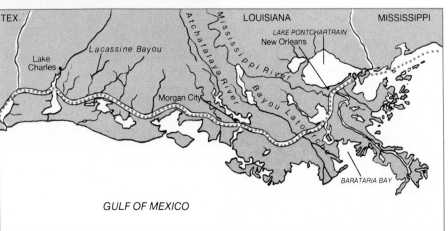

Laguna Madre

Few cruising grounds present such relaxing opportunities for clear-ahead passage-making as 120-mile-long Laguna Madre on the Texas Gulf Coast. A boatman procedes along this lightly traveled channel, 12 feet deep and 125 feet wide, with all the ease of a jet pilot cruising clear skies. Purple and ocher mud flats line the western bank, while to seaward rise the glistening white dunes of Padre Island, a thin strip of sand shielding this stretch of the Gulf Waterway from southeast winds.

At the lagoon's northern end, opposite the oil port of Corpus Christi Harbor, motels and marinas crowd the tip of Padre Island. Just below this busy roadstead the boatman can mosey in sunlit peace, trolling for sea trout and redfish in the company of the 350 species of wild fowl that inhabit or visit the area. But he must remember that all the way down to Port Isabel at the lagoon's southern end, the only supply points are the fishing hamlets at Baffin Bay and Port Mansfield.

Padre Island fairly begs to be explored. A skipper with a diligent eye on the chart can find anchorages all along it. For example, opposite Port Mansfield, where a channel cuts through the island to the gulf, he can moor just inside one of the flanking jetties. Most of Padre Island is undeveloped national seashore. Its sandy hills, dotted with wind-stunted brush and sea oats, are open to campers. Its shell-strewn beaches look much as they did when, in 1553, a convoy of loot-laden Spanish galleons was driven ashore here in a gale. Divers have recovered some of the treasure, but visitors have little chance to take home a sea-smoothed doubloon, since the state of Texas claims all such finds. Still, anyone can come away with a pocketful of shiny shells and imperishable memories of sea, sand, sun and solitude.

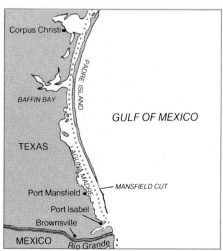

The waters of the Gulf of Mexico foam against an empty beach
curving over the horizon in this southward-looking view of Padre
Island. Shallow pools left by a recent storm shimmer at the feet of
wind-swept dunes that rise to heights of 30 feet or more. To the right,
on the landward side of this narrow barrier, lies the calm expanse of
Laguna Madre, a 120-mile link in the Intracoastal Waterway between
Corpus Christi and Port Isabel near the Mexican border.

8

It was just before dawn, and I was standing on the very tip of the bowsprit, clutching the jibstay. There was a sibilant hiss from the bow wave as the ketch *Temptress* heeled to a warm southeasterly breeze. An occasional crest slapped against the topsides to glitter in the running lights. Looking aloft, I watched the mast weave patterns against the stars, which seemed no more remote than the Gulf Stream pursuing its mysterious way beneath our keel. We had left Fort Lauderdale at dusk, and somewhere ahead lay my first glimpse of the islands that spray out in a lazy arc from the doorstep of Florida to Trinidad on the shoulder of South America. Gradually I realized the night was becoming

THE CARIBBEAN ISLANDS

less dark. The stars paled, and a faint glow appeared in the east. I strained to see, and there on the horizon was silhouetted our first landfall: the Bahamian islands of Bimini. It was Christmas Eve 1932, and I have never forgotten the magic of that moment.

The ensuing moments remain just as vividly in my mind: the wondrous palette of dawn on the fringe of the tropical sky—yellow, rose, crimson and, finally, an incandescent burst as the sun climbed clear, transmuting the black night sea into a spectrum of colors. The ocean astern became a rich indigo, while ahead the shallow waters paled into cool pastels, every shade of blue and green, until they lapped against a sand beach of purest white. Judging the contours and depth of the bottom by the water hues, my skipper conned us into harbor, where we dropped anchor and basked in the inner content that comes after an ocean passage, no matter how short.

Since then it has been my good fortune to make many landfalls in many parts of the world, always recapturing a bit of the excitement of that first moment off Bimini. Yet no matter where I go, I feel no other cruising area is so blessed as the one that is speckled with those southern islands that Columbus, thinking he had arrived off the coast of Asia, lumped together as "West Indies." Strictly speaking, the islands divide into two major groups. The Bahamas, where Columbus made his first landfall, are lapped by the Gulf Stream and lie fully within the Atlantic Ocean. The second tier, comprising the Greater and Lesser Antilles, spills nearly 2,000 miles across the belt of trade winds and marks the boundary of the Caribbean.

Within these two island groups the variety of landforms and character is infinite, ranging from the low barren cays to towering volcanic peaks swathed in lush tropic rain forests, and peopled by a potpourri of nationalities and races from Europe, Africa and Asia. For a sailor with romance in his bones, the sea becomes a tapestry woven by the keels of vanished ships, once manned by explorers, colonists, merchants, buccaneers, soldiers, missionaries, farmers and just plain folk, who were inspired by hope, by greed, by faith, by lust—driven, in fact, by every motive and dream that could prompt a streaming of life to what was literally a New World. Perhaps the one common denominator of the islands is excellence of climate. Despite some minor seasonal variations, there is probably no more equable and agreeable year-round weather anywhere on this planet.

For most yachtsmen crossing the Gulf Stream from the States, the Bahamas are the first landfall, as they were for me. Bimini and Grand Bahama are within 60 miles of the coast of Florida; the others extend about 750 miles southeast, straddling the Tropic of Cancer. The Bahamas, some 3,000 islands, cays and lesser outcroppings, have only one drawback, from my point of view. I am a barefoot beachcomber as well as a sailor, and in winter the Bahamas are subject to occasional northers, the final flick of the tails of blizzards sweeping across the snowbound United States. For a few days at a time,

A chartered ketch rides at anchor within swimming distance of Stocking Island off Great Exuma. Here the water is so clear that a cruising skipper can see the bottom at 30 feet.

Carleton Mitchell has explored virtually every cruising area in the world from the Baltic to the South Pacific, but the Caribbean—as he has avowed in three books and countless articles—ranks as his lifelong love.

temperatures may drop to wool-shirt weather—about 50°. But such days are the exception; there is never any frost, and the average winter temperature is a deliciously balmy 70.

Two physical phenomena combine to make Bahamian cruising unique. First are the formations called banks, sandy plateaus stretching for thousands of square miles, submerged at an average depth of only several fathoms. Second is the clarity of the water, which may be equaled in a few favored parts of the world, but nowhere is excelled. Picture the most limpid water you ever saw—a swimming pool freshly filled, a mountain pool fed by springs; then imagine it spread thin over white sand patterned by coral heads, grassy patches and deep channels. Pilotage, as I learned on that first approach long ago, is not so much a matter of reading charts as it is reading water colors—dark blue means relatively deep water, shading to turquoise then to lettuce green in the shallows. But almost anywhere the bottom is sufficiently close so that the anchor can be dropped at will. The islands themselves are low limestone formations. Typical is Great Inagua, where rosy-hued flamingos stalk against snow-white mounds of salt—a major export that is harvested from the sea in shallow evaporation pans and left to bleach in the sun.

The southeastern Bahamas form stepping stones to the Greater Antilles, below which lie the gentle waters of the Caribbean. The first cruising stop is Hispaniola—lovely name!—the island shared by Haiti and the Dominican Republic. Bold shores rise tier on tier to 10,000-foot forested mountains, their tops usually swathed in a trade-wind cumulus. On these slopes in Columbus' time, the Indians burned beacon fires to warn friends of approaching raiders. Columbus found Hispaniola fit "for everything in the world that man can want," and named one site that he explored Valle del Paraiso (Valley of Paradise). But harbors in Haiti are few, and offshore seas rough. And while I once spent a delightful winter exploring the Gulf of Gonave in western Haiti, and later circumnavigated Jamaica and pre-Castro Cuba, I must confess that for me the Greater Antilles have always been passage islands, to be visited mainly for shelter and supplies.

East of Hispaniola, past Puerto Rico, lies a minicluster of islands I always think of as a separate cruising ground. These are the Virgins, which form a protective natural breakwater of islets and reefs—where centuries ago at least one unwary gold-laden Spanish galleon sank. Inside the reefs, however, winds are fresh but the sea never builds. The runs are short, with no more than an hour or two between most harbors, and anchorages are snug.

Then, due east of the Virgins comes that perfect necklace of islands, the wonderful 500-mile-long crescent listed on charts as the Lesser Antilles. They lie scattered in the sea, as though they were indeed gems tossed away by a careless pirate. Here are the warmest, the lushest, the most picturesque and the most internationally flavored of the islands in the Caribbean. Spanish, English, Dutch, French, Danish, Scottish, Swedish and African settlers have spiced the towns with their languages, their customs, their architecture and crafts. Civilization has brought fine restaurants with bright lights and maîtres d'hôtel who bow deeply from the waist. Still, nature has left a bonanza of lonely anchorages and untrodden beaches.

To my mind, the cruising in the Lesser Antilles is the finest to be had anywhere. All the way south from Anguilla to Grenada, peaks lift from the sea ahead as others drop astern; there are gentle arcs and jagged cones, live volcanoes and tangled rain forests ablaze with tropical flowers. The trade winds on the beam make for dazzling, effortless swoops across the deep blue channels, which are protected from ocean swells by the island chain. Yet, here and there at breaks in the chain, the Atlantic rushes in to keep a sailor on his mettle. Indeed, water, land and wind are exquisitely arranged as though a beneficent providence, during creation of this quarter of the world, had sailors specifically in mind.

by Carleton Mitchell

Antigua's English Harbour is perhaps the finest anchorage in all the
Caribbean and has served as a mariner's refuge for more than three
centuries. It was a key refitting base for the British Navy during the
18th and 19th centuries, and Horatio Nelson, as a fledgling sea captain
in the 1780s, threaded its narrow entryway in his frigate, H.M.S.
Boreas. The old naval base has been restored and supplemented by
facilities for modern yachtsmen—fresh water, fuel, showers and a
charter brokerage. But boatmen should enter cautiously: the harbor
approaches are ill-marked and should not be attempted at night.

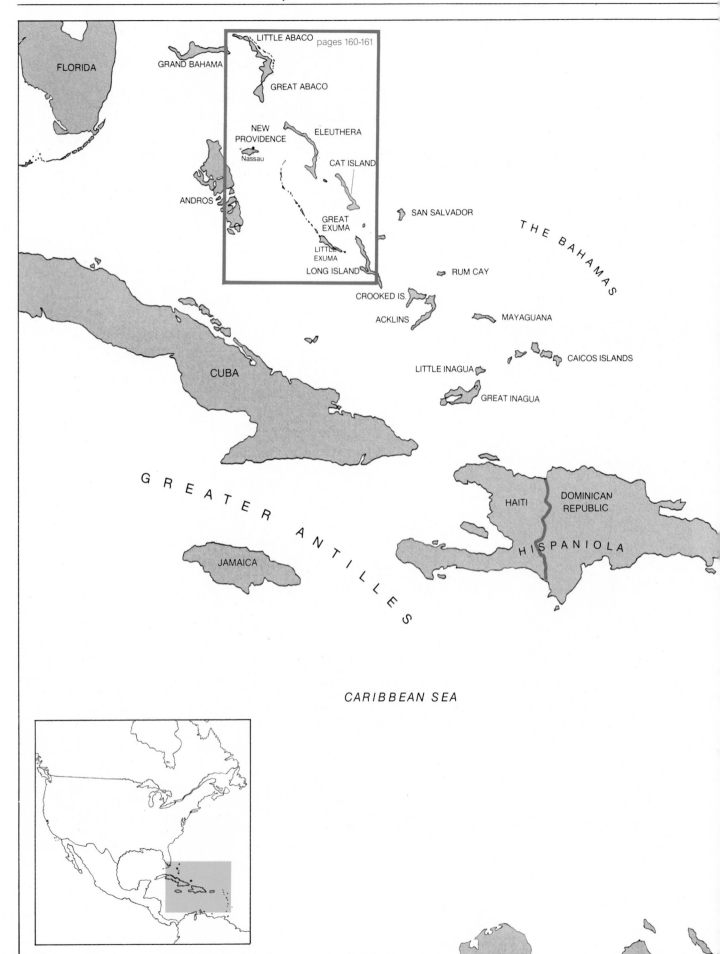

pages 160-161

LITTLE ABACO

GRAND BAHAMA

GREAT ABACO

FLORIDA

NEW
PROVIDENCE

Nassau

ELEUTHERA

CAT ISLAND

ANDROS

SAN SALVADOR

T H E   B A H A M A S

GREAT
EXUMA

LITTLE
EXUMA

LONG ISLAND

RUM CAY

CROOKED IS.

ACKLINS

MAYAGUANA

CAICOS ISLANDS

CUBA

LITTLE INAGUA

GREAT INAGUA

G R E A T E R   A N T I L L E S

HAITI

DOMINICAN
REPUBLIC

H I S P A N I O L A

JAMAICA

CARIBBEAN SEA

Bridge of Islands

The curved bridge of islands that arcs between North and South America is made up of the summits of a vast undersea mountain range, longer than the Appalachians and almost as high in places as the Rockies. In the massif's northern tier, white limestone plateaus called banks, thousands of square miles in size, rise more than 10,000 feet above the ocean floor. The portions of the banks that break the water's surface are the Bahama Islands, a prime cruising ground focused around Nassau on the central island of New Providence. From Nassau, a universe of satellite islands, from tiny, nameless outcroppings to sprawling Abaco and Exuma, lie within a long day's run.

Below the Bahamas rise the massive volcanic forms of Hispaniola—the island that incorporates Haiti and the Dominican Republic—and Puerto Rico. In contrast to their low-lying scrub-covered neighbors, the Greater Antilles—Hispaniola, Jamaica, Cuba and Puerto Rico—are mantled in lush jungles rising in some places a full 8,000 feet above sea level. During the 1960s and early '70s, volatile political climates on several of these islands caused yachtsmen to steer clear. But as late as the mid-'50s, they were great favorites, and by the mid-'70s their splendid deepwater harbors were once again luring adventurous boatmen.

Just east of Puerto Rico lie the Virgins, half U.S., half British—and all hospitable to visiting sailors. Higher than the Bahamas and with generally deep water offshore, these islands stand so close together that runs between harbors are short —sometimes only an hour or two.

Curving southeast from the Virgin Islands, and eventually southwest toward South America, are the sheer peaks, the cloud-capped summits and small crescent beaches of the Lesser Antilles. Volcanic in origin, the islands are lower and generally smaller toward the north; in fact, Anguilla and Barbuda were once sea-covered, and their surfaces are made up of brilliant white coral growths. Here the runs between ports tend to be a bit longer, and cruising skippers are careful to stay to the west of the islands, protected from the sweep of Atlantic combers that crash against the rocky eastern shores.

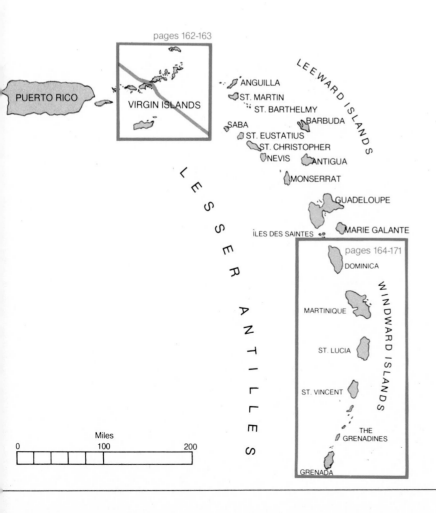

Winds and Weather

As far north as Nassau, midwinter temperatures average an ideal 72°. An occasional cold blast of arctic air may chill the Bahamas and Greater Antilles to a brisk 50°, but no part of the region ever experiences a frost. Heat waves over 90° are almost equally unusual; 1,000 miles south of the Bahamas on the island of Grenada, August days generally stay below 85°.

Rain in the West Indies comes in violent bursts that rarely last longer than an hour, except in the islands' highest rain forests. These brief showers cut visibility, as does intermittent mist. Real fog is unknown, however, and overall the sea air here has unusual clarity—from the deck of a cruising boat it is not unusual to be able to see a mountaintop 40 miles away.

Trade winds blow constantly from across the Atlantic. In winter, they bluster in from the northeast at a steady 15 to 20 knots; from late January through February, winter winds may pipe up to 25 to 30 knots for days on end. In summer, the breeze veers around to the southeast, gentling off to 8 to 12 knots. Throughout the year, the trades normally become strongest at about two in the afternoon. Occasionally, a squall strong enough to force a sailor to shorten sail funnels down the slopes of a mountainous island, or a thunderstorm packs a 50-mile-per-hour punch.

There is one very real danger from the weather in this area: the Caribbean is a spawning ground for tropical storms that sweep north through the islands and occasionally reach hurricane force as they head for the eastern seaboard of the United States. Fortunately, nearly all hurricanes occur between August and October, and most of them can be predicted early enough to give a sailor a head start to shelter.

Tides and Currents

No natural force in the West Indies is more certain than the direction of the prevailing currents, nor less certain than the duration and timing of the tides. The major current that washes the shores of all the West Indian islands is a branch of the north equatorial current, sweeping westward from the Atlantic. As it reaches Central America, it arcs northward, circulates to the east through the Gulf of Mexico and exits by passing at two to three knots between Florida and the Bahamas, where it joins the Gulf Stream. Local currents throughout the Caribbean are almost all adjustments to this overall pattern, though they are influenced by regional geography and local winds and storms.

Although the tidal range in the West Indies is small—less than three feet—predicting the times of the tides is difficult. In the Bahamas, tides rise and ebb twice daily; each high tide is approximately the same height as the last. In the Virgins, tides flood and ebb only once, although certain local variations produce as many as four daily. Toward South America, tides become mixed, rising twice a day but to unequal heights.

Tidal currents in the West Indies flood to the east at between one and two knots and ebb westerly at two to three knots. A flood tide setting against the trades and equatorial current frequently produces a stomach-churning chop.

Pilotage

The clarity of the air and the transparency of the waters make piloting the West Indies all but effortless and hazard-free in a shallow-draft boat. Individual underwater obstacles can easily be seen and avoided. Practically all snags or reefs in the West Indies are either coral or coral-encrusted, and appear pale or whitish green, or deep brown when they are overgrown with seaweed.

Salad-green stretches of sea, on the other hand, mean safe cruising in depths of 10 feet or more. Laying a compass course here is essential only for legs of 15 miles or more. A skipper who knows the region is likely to pick out a mountaintop or a palm-studded islet on the horizon and head for it, while watching out for telltale color changes in the water that signal trouble ahead. Failure to keep a sharp lookout may bring a resounding crunch and a layover in a boatyard.

West Indian waters are not very well marked, and those buoys that do exist conform to a number of different buoyage systems. Puerto Rico and the Virgins are marked according to the United States system—i.e., red, right, returning. British and French waters, which include the Windward and Leeward islands areas, adhere to the International Uniform System of Buoyage that is completely opposite to the U.S. system—in effect, black, right, returning. The Bahamas have a system of their own that consists primarily of marking an obstruction directly by erecting a spar atop it. Warning: Do not run at night. There are few lighted buoys in the Indies—and they are often allowed to burn out.

Boats and Special Equipment

The easiest way to cruise the West Indies is by bareboat charter (no professional captain or crew aboard). The company stocks the boat with the basic equipment needed for cruising: sails, charts, linen, blankets, cooking utensils—in some places, even snorkeling and fishing gear. The skipper usually must supply his own food and drink, but for a price some charter companies will do so. Charter-boat cruises are usually round-trip operations; but for a fee, a drop-off point can be settled upon. Bareboat charter prices range from about $300 to more than $1,000 a week, with a refundable deposit of one third the fee to help insure against boat damage. Charter boats should be booked early; the Christmas season is sometimes sold out a year in advance.

Skippers who cruise their own boats to the West Indies should bring along a wind scoop to keep the cabin comfortable on muggy nights. When a boat is anchored or moving under the engine by day, a cockpit canopy is a necessity for guarding against sunburn. A dinghy hoisted aboard or towed astern extends a cruiser's exploring range over shallow banks and reefs, particularly if the tender is coupled with a powerful outboard.

Wildlife

The West Indies are prime territory for bird watchers. Among the most numerous species are the Virgin Islands pelicans and the candy-colored Bahamas flamingos. Fine additions to any life list are the rare sisserou parrots of Dominica and the Martinique kingfishers. Reptiles also flourish in the islands, including four species of giant turtle: the green, hawksbill, loggerhead and ridley. And practically all of the islands are alive with lizards, from giant iguanas to tiny chameleons. Mammals are scarce; the only large ones are the deer in the highlands of St. Thomas and St. Croix. In the rain forest an explorer might find a monkey swinging overhead or a possum sleeping in a treetop. The snake-killing mongoose lives on many southern islands; unfortunately, owing to a scarcity of snakes, the mongoose hunts birds.

Sports

The West Indies have long been a favored region for salt-water fishermen. Prime quarry ranges from sleek bonefish on the Bahama Banks (a world-record 16-pounder was taken there) to half-ton blue marlin. Even boatmen with no real interest in fishing might bring along a rod with a four- to eight-pound test line just to hang over the side; a few bareboat charterers chip in a rod and tackle. Some of the most prolific waters are those lapping the Bahamas, particularly Cat Cay, Bimini, Walker's Cay and the offshore environs of Nassau. Here kingfish, wahoo, bonito and tuna abound; white and blue marlin and an occasional sailfish are also pulled in. The same game fish also occur in relative abundance around Puerto Rico and the Lesser Antilles.

The snorkeling and scuba diving in the West Indies are every bit as spectacular as conventional fishing. Outstanding shallow-water spots, teeming with tropical fish and often harboring a wreck or two, exist in the Tobago Cays in the Grenadines, the whole Virgin archipelago, especially Horse Shoe Reef, and the coral heads that rise from the Bahama Banks.

Regional Boating Regulations

Since the West Indies are divided up among nearly a dozen countries, a cruising boat spends a fair amount of time passing through customs. Though there are some minor variations from island to island, the general procedure is to land at a port of entry listed in the cruising guides or *Sailing Directions*. While entering the harbor, hoist the yellow code flag "Q" (meaning quarantined), tie up at a dock and wait for a customs inspector. Leaving the boat is against the law in some places, even for the skipper. Show the inspector the ship's papers, the clearance certificate from the last port of departure, the crew list and positive individual identification, such as a birth certificate. Passports are not usually required but are certain to be accepted. In some countries, like Haiti, it is considered good form to extend hospitality to the customs officials; offer them a beer. And it is customary in most West Indian countries to fly the appropriate courtesy flag from the starboard spreader or radio antenna; frequently, flags may be purchased from the customs inspectors.

Major Provisioning Ports

Unless otherwise noted, the following list of principal West Indies ports describes those that provide the widest range of supplies and services, including fuel and water pumps or trucks, food stores and basic repair facilities. The ports are close to towns or cities where the boatman can find medical services and telephone or telegraph connections.

Nassau: On the island of New Providence, the only full-service Bahamian port. Mathew Town, Great Inagua, ranks a faraway second but provides a convenient jump-off point for cruises to the Caicos Islands, Hispaniola or Puerto Rico.

Port-au-Prince: The capital of Haiti and the major commercial port of Hispaniola, with few repair facilities for small boats. Better to run to La Romana on the southern coast of the Dominican Republic.

San Juan: One of the oldest and largest ports of all the West Indies, with complete facilities for both commercial vessels and pleasure craft. Its entrance is easily negotiated, even at night, which makes it a perfect emergency shelter.

St. Thomas Harbor: The principal port of both the U.S. and British Virgin Islands. The other U.S. Virgin Islands port is Christiansted, on St. Croix.

Road Town: On Tortola, the only full-service port in the British Virgins.

English Harbour: On Antigua (page 155), the safest

and coziest small-boat harbor in the Leewards. Guadaloupe's Pointe-à-Pitre is a bustling commercial waterfront, better equipped for difficult repairs than English Harbour, but much less attractive.

St. George's: The capital of Grenada (pages 170-171) and the southernmost port in the Windwards. It ranks in size with Roseau on Dominica, Castries on St. Lucia and Fort-de-France, Martinique.

Coast Guard Stations

The only U.S. Coast Guard station in the West Indies is in San Juan, Puerto Rico. It has jurisdiction over the waters of Puerto Rico and adjacent United States islands. No equivalent to the U.S. Coast Guard operates elsewhere in the Caribbean.

Charts and Publications

National Ocean Survey charts range from the 26000 series for the Bahamas and Hispaniola to the 25000 series for Puerto Rico and the Lesser Antilles. The British Admiralty and French Hydrographic Service also produce charts for the Lesser Antilles; these may be used for cross-checking in conjunction with the NOS charts for the corresponding areas since no chart is absolutely accurate in all cases.

Aids to navigation in the U.S. West Indies (Puerto Rico and the U.S. Virgins) are catalogued in Volume II of the light lists, entitled *Atlantic and Gulf Coast*. National Ocean Survey tide tables for the east coasts of North and South America apply generally to the West Indies. Specific tables do not exist for many localities—where tides are, in any case, slight and variable.

The U.S. Naval Oceanographic Office publishes two volumes of *Sailing Directions for the West Indies*: Volume I for Bermuda, the Bahamas and the Greater Antilles; Volume II for the Lesser Antilles and Venezuela. They contain information ranging from oceanography and climate to buoyage, clearing customs and procedures for entering unfamiliar ports. The most recent revisions of charts can be obtained in principal ports. U.S. charts may be purchased from these government agencies:

Defense Mapping Agency Depot
5801 Tabor Avenue
Philadelphia, Pennsylvania 19120

National Ocean Survey
Distribution Division, C44
6501 Lafayette Avenue
Riverdale, Maryland 20840

The following publications are especially valuable for specific information on small harbors, anchorages and useful facilities:

Kline, Harry, ed.:
Yachtsman's Guide to the Bahamas. Tropic Isle Publishers, Inc.
Yachtsman's Guide to the Virgin Islands, Puerto Rico, Republic of Haiti, Dominican Republic. Tropic Isle Publishers, Inc.
Rickards, Colin, ed., *The West Indies and Caribbean Year Book.* Caribook, Ltd.
Street, Donald M., Jr., *A Cruising Guide to the Lesser Antilles.* Sail Books, Inc.
Van Ost, John R., ed., *Yachtsman's Guide to the Windward Islands.* CSY, Inc.

The Bahamas

The white and windswept islands of the Bahama archipelago, jutting above shallow waters that cover the Great and Little Bahama banks, bake in the sun like rocky outcroppings on a desert. And, in fact, with their patches of scrubgrass and widespread lack of running water, the Bahamas do have a kinship with some desert areas. But the relationship is by no means close; the ample rain showers and warm Atlantic waters that wash these islands have made them a lush cruising ground.

Most Bahama Banks cruises take off from New Providence, the hub of the archipelago and site of its major city, Nassau. Here two profound trenches, the Tongue of the Ocean and Exuma Sound, slash into the west and east through thousands of square miles of surrounding shallows. When heading off from Nassau to another island, a skipper may expect a little rough going as he takes on the ocean swells of these mile-deep trenches.

Just beyond, however, an almost unlimited number of fair-weather hideaways wait to be discovered in the out-island cruising grounds—from Pipe Creek's labyrinth of cays *(right)* southeast of Nassau to the Abacos 60 miles north. In the sprawling shallows between, bonefish abound, growing to world-record weights of 15 pounds. The swimming and snorkeling in the Bahamas is unexcelled anywhere in the Western Hemisphere: the water is a balmy 78°, and multicolored fish flock in droves near coral heads crowned with sponges and sea anemones.

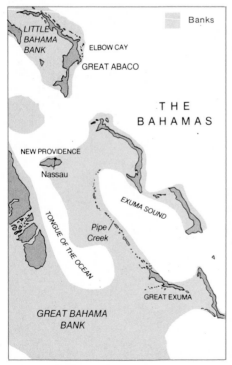

Pipe Creek, actually a secluded archipelago, comprises 17 cays —including Rat Cay, left—and hundreds of unnamed rocks. The maze of bights and channels between the rocks and cays provides safe anchorage almost anywhere, regardless of wind direction. Most of Pipe Creek's limestone hummocks are uninhabited, but Staniel Cay has a settlement where yachtsmen can purchase anything from groceries to scuba gear. It also has a medical clinic, an airstrip and a fairly well-equipped marina. In addition, the Staniel Cay Yacht Club offers guest cottages by reservation to all comers.

Workboats tied up to a downtown pier in Nassau unload produce at the open-air market along Woodes Rogers Walk. Here yachtsmen can stock up on oranges, bananas, coconuts, fish, conchs, limes and crabs. Behind the market lies Nassau's complex of first-class restaurants, boutiques and hotels. And up and down the channel on either side are marinas and boatyards that can handle yachts of any size.

A three-masted schooner rides at anchor in Elbow Cay's Hope Town Harbour. Overlooking the harbor, Elbow Cay Light guides approaching boats past the edge of Little Bahama Bank on the northernmost coast of the Bahamas. Before the lighthouse was constructed in the mid-19th Century, some enterprising inhabitants of Hope Town supplemented their incomes by building false beacon fires on the bank to lure merchant vessels to their doom. The people were obstinately opposed to the lighthouse—understandably so, since wrecking produced incomes of up to 112,000 pounds sterling a year.

A chartered 65-foot staysail schooner beats against northeasterly
trades in the 100-foot-deep waters of Sir Francis Drake Channel, the
major cruising highway of the British Virgins. The channel, extending
15 miles between St. John (background, above) and Virgin Gorda, is
named for the Elizabethan freebooter who sailed through here in
1595 on his way to attack the Spanish settlement of San Juan.

The Virgins

When Christopher Columbus first sighted the Virgin Islands in 1493, he saw a string of mountaintops that he assumed rose from a single large land mass. But as he drew near he discovered that the summits crowned the islands of a miniature archipelago. Columbus claimed the clustered isles for Spain, and named them the Virgins after the legend of St. Ursula, who went to sea and ultimately perished with a company of 10,999 maidens.

Today, ownership of the 100 or so islands and islets that make up the Virgins is divided between the United States and Great Britain. To cruise them, most skippers fly out from the mainland and then charter a boat, either at U.S.-administered St. Thomas or at British Tortola.

From either point, setting a course here is a simple matter of picking out the right summit and steering for it. There is never any fog. Tides are generally less than a foot, and a skipper entering a harbor can pilot his way between reefs and coral heads by looking through the clear Caribbean water. And ports are so close together that the only jump of any length between neighboring harbors is the 35-mile crossing from St. Thomas south to St. Croix. Perhaps the best all-round sailing is in the British group—up the broad, sheltered avenue of Sir Francis Drake Channel *(left)*, with the island peaks rising majestically beside the channel.

Throughout these beguiling islands are coves and beaches where a skipper can drop his hook for a swim, a quiet lunch or a solitary sunbath. The coral shoals hold ancient wrecks where rainbows of tropical fish glint in the sea-filtered sunlight. The snorkeling is superb around Anegada's Horse Shoe Reef, the Virgin Gorda Baths *(top right)* and the caves of Norman Island—Robert Louis Stevenson's Treasure Island, where the pirate Mr. Fleming is said to have cached his coffers of gold.

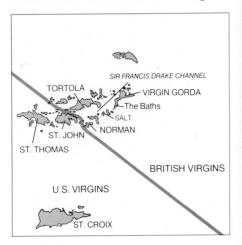

Giant granite boulders—some of them 40 feet high—form a labyrinth of grottoes called The Baths at the southwest tip of Virgin Gorda. Awash at their base and lighted from above by shafts of sun, The Baths provide a unique arena for rock scrambling and swimming. Snorkeling aficionados go for coral just off the beach. Warning: the holding ground here is poor and the surge strong. For an overnight berth, a skipper should go north one and a half miles to the marina near Spanish Town.

Squirrelfish—one of more than 300 species of reef fish to be found in the Virgins—dart near the sunken superstructure of the British mail liner Rhone, which foundered on the southwest point of Salt Island in 1867. Nearby Lee Bay provides a temporary anchorage for divers exploring the wreck. But here, too, boats should seek a quiet haven before nightfall—in Norman Island's Bight or in one of Peter Island's three protected anchorages.

Dominica's north-shore bluffs rise beneath a mantle of wind-blown tropical scrub. Beyond the headland, a dense rain forest ascends to the island's perpetually cloud-covered mountaintops; the highest, Morne Diablotin, reaches 4,747 feet. A primitive road cuts into Dominica's northern regions, making this sector of the wilderness partially accessible, either on foot or in jeeps that can be rented in Roseau, the island's main port.

The tangled roots of the bloodwood tree sink into Dominica's coastal swampland area, which can be reached from the shore by dinghy. The swamps are fed by the island's extraordinarily heavy rainfall, which varies from 70 inches annually on the coast to an incredible 200 or more inches in the upper mountains. Dominica's dank climate supports banana and mahogany trees, as well as grapefruits, limes, pineapples and breadfruit.

DOMINICA

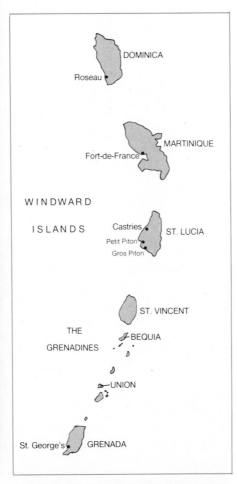

The Windwards

No island group in all the Caribbean provides such varied and challenging cruising as the southern stretch of the Lesser Antilles. These lofty crests, designated on charts as the Windward Islands, march southward in an orderly, even-spaced progression. For much of their length, the cruising channels are calm and relatively protected, but in some stretches the boatman must be ready for lively sailing.

For example, a skipper can make an early departure from the banana wharfs of Roseau on the northernmost island in the chain, Dominica, with its cloud-capped peaks cloaked in virgin jungle. As he moves out from the lee of the island, he must brace for five or six hours of rough slogging as he crosses the passage to Martinique. Here he is exposed to the full force of the northeast trades, as well as a mean swell rolling in from the Atlantic. Then, as he slides into the shelter of Martinique, the seas level off, the wind dies —and if he heads too close inshore he may find himself becalmed in the lee of the shoreside peaks.

On reaching Martinique, most skippers put in at St. Pierre on the island's northern end and then move down the coast the following morning a scant 15 miles to the civilized Gallic pleasures of Fort-de-France. Martinique is an overseas department of France, with a strong Creole spicing, and here visitors will find superb French cooking, fine calypso music and a small-scale version of the Sacré Coeur basilica *(overleaf)*.

Next down the chain lies St. Lucia, a British possession with a partially French heritage. The two nations battled for more than a century over the island before it was finally ceded to Great Britain in 1815. Fortifications still crown the slopes of 852-foot-high Morne Fortune, a five-minute taxi ride from the main harbor at Castries.

South of St. Lucia, the resolutely Anglican St. Vincent provides a convenient jump-off spot for a cruise through the Grenadines, which many Caribbean enthusiasts consider to be the most beautiful sailing ground in the Windwards. Here the islands are closer together than in the rest of the Windwards, and they offer a plenitude of short day sails to convenient and secluded anchorages.

At their southern terminus sits Grenada and its bustling harbor of St. George's, once likened to the Mediterranean haven Portofino. With its abundance of ship and small-boat supplies, restaurants, and hotels, St. George's makes a perfect spot to end—or begin—a cruise.

The red-necked parrot, or Jaquot, inhabits the upper reaches of the island's rain forest, though in recent years its numbers have been drastically cut through overhunting. Not only does the brightly hued bird fetch high prices in pet shops, but its succulent flesh is a favored delicacy in native stewpots. Still plentiful in the island's jungle are such tropical exotica as iguanas and giant frogs called crapauds, which weigh up to two pounds and taste like chicken.

THE WINDWARDS: MARTINIQUE

A small flotilla of Martinique's fishing canoes —called gommiers—lies tethered in the Rivière Madame, a busy canal leading into the native market at Fort-de-France. With outboard motors astern and double spars at the bow for setting square spritsails, these canoes transport the island's 2,000 fishermen as far as 20 miles out to sea in search of snapper, mullet, grouper and dozens of other fish. Beyond the arching bridge in the distance is the Anchorage des Flamands, where charter yachts, banana boats, trading schooners and even a 600-foot cruise ship or two can swing comfortably at anchor.

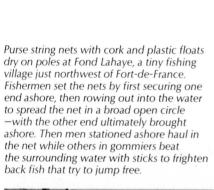

Purse string nets with cork and plastic floats dry on poles at Fond Lahaye, a tiny fishing village just northwest of Fort-de-France. Fishermen set the nets by first securing one end ashore, then rowing out into the water to spread the net in a broad open circle —with the other end ultimately brought ashore. Then men stationed ashore haul in the net while others in gommiers beat the surrounding water with sticks to frighten back fish that try to jump free.

A small-scale replica of the Paris basilica of Sacré Coeur gleams in the lush vegetation of Balata, a village three miles north of Fort-de-France. Clearly visible from more than 10 miles offshore, the basilica makes a convenient landmark when approaching the harbor from the westerly quarter.

One of the open-air markets at Fort-de-France occupies a block-sized square at the corner of Rue Isambert and Rue Siger. Here Martiniquaise women gather every morning in the week except Sunday to bargain in Creole patois for oranges, pineapples, mangoes, root vegetables, papayas and anthurium blooms. The market is accessible from the port by dinghy through the Rivière Madame (opposite at top), making it an ideal restocking place for cruisers.

THE WINDWARDS: ST. LUCIA

Like a pair of enormous fangs, two ancient volcanic cones—Petit and Gros Piton—loom 2,461 and 2,619 feet respectively above St. Lucia's southwest shore. Beneath their summits in the spectacular harbor of Anse des Pitons the bottom drops away so precipitously that, to moor, a sailor must tie up to a palm tree ashore and set an anchor astern.

The palm- and mango-fringed arms of Marigot Harbor, halfway up the west coast of St. Lucia, embrace two moored charter boats. Marigot is an all-weather haven—one of the few in the Caribbean that is safe even in a hurricane. So effectively is the harbor enclosed, in fact, that a British fleet once evaded a pursuing French force by ducking into the lagoon (left) and disguising their rigging with palm fronds.

THE WINDWARDS: THE GRENADINES

Pink-and-white stucco houses tumble down the sides of the flooded volcano crater that forms the harbor of St. George's in Grenada —south of the Grenadines. Marine-supply depots, clothing and food stores, and the largest full-service marina in the Windward Islands lie at the harbor's edge. The deepwater anchorage in the foreground —called the Carenage—is reserved for charter boats, fishing craft and freighters. Small boats anchor in a protected basin to the southeast.

A small sand cay shields the entrance to Clifton Harbor, a convenient supply port on Union Island in the Middle Grenadines. The cay's five palm trees are permanently canted to the south by the constant force of the trade winds, which in this part of the Windwards tend to blow in from north to northeast at up to 25 knots. The entire stretch of the Grenadines is strewn with such tiny cays, and sailors should keep a sharp eye peeled for them; many of them project no more than a foot or two above the surface of the water.

A rude wooden monument to native mariners lost at sea overlooks the main harbor in Admiralty Bay in Bequia, northernmost of the Grenadines. The island's seamen—principally of Scottish descent—still harpoon whales in the surrounding waters from their six-man, double-ended whale boats. Pleasure boats entering Admiralty Bay should stay well clear of a rock-strewn headland called Devil's Table to the north of the entrance. Once in, like the trading schooners shown here, they can anchor safely in hard sand.

Further Reading

The Pacific Northwest

American Marine Directory & Boaters Handbook, Pacific Northwest Division. Northwest Maritime Publications, 1973.

Binns, Archie, *Northwest Gateway*. Binfords & Mort, 1941.

Federal Writers' Project, *Washington*. Somerset Publishers, reprint of 1941 edition.

Kelsey, Vera, *British Columbia Rides a Star*. Harper & Brothers, 1958.

California and Mexico's Baja

Beautiful California, by the editorial staffs of Sunset Books and *Sunset* magazine. Lane Book Company, 1963.

Cannon, Ray, and the *Sunset* editors, *The Sea of Cortez*. Lane Magazine & Book Company, 1966.

Johnson, William Weber, and the editors of TIME-LIFE Books, *Baja California*. Time Inc., 1972.

Kelley, Don Greame, *Edge of a Continent*. American West Publishing Company, 1971.

Krutch, Joseph Wood, *The Forgotten Peninsula*. William Morrow & Company, Inc., 1961.

Miller, Tom, and Elmar Baxter, *The Baja Book*. Baja Trail Publications, 1974.

Simpson, Lesley B., *Many Mexicos*. University of California Press, 1966.

Steinbeck, John, and E. F. Ricketts, *The Log from the Sea of Cortez*. Bantam Books, Inc., 1971.

The California Missions, by the editorial staff of Sunset Books. Lane Book Company, 1964.

Cruising Rivers of America

Banta, R. E., *The Ohio*. The Rivers of America. Rinehart & Company, 1949.

Cabell, Branch, and A. J. Hanna, *The St. Johns*. The Rivers of America. Farrar & Rinehart, Inc., 1943.

Carmer, Carl Lamson, *The Hudson River*. Holt, Rinehart & Winston, Inc., 1974.

Carter, Hodding, *Lower Mississippi*. The Rivers of America. Farrar & Rinehart, Inc., 1942.

Dana, Julian, *Sacramento, River of Gold*. Scholarly Press, 1971.

Davidson, Donald, *Tennessee*. The Rivers of America. Holt, Rinehart & Winston, Inc., 1946.

DeVoto, Bernard, *The Journals of Lewis & Clark*. Houghton Mifflin Company, 1953.

Havighurst, Walter, *Upper Mississippi*. The Rivers of America. Farrar & Rinehart, Inc., 1937.

Keating, Bern, *The Mighty Mississippi*. The National Geographic Society, 1971.

McCague, James, *The Cumberland*. Holt, Rinehart & Winston, Inc., 1973.

McDowell, Robert Emmett, *Re-discovering Kentucky*. Kentucky Department of Parks, 1971.

Powell, J. W., *The Exploration of the Colorado River and Its Canyons*. Dover Publications, Inc., 1961.

Twain, Mark, *Life on the Mississippi*. Harper & Row, 1965.

Vestal, Stanley, *The Missouri*. The Rivers of America. Farrar & Rinehart, Inc., 1945.

Walters, Robert E., *Cruising the California Delta*. Miller Freeman Publications, Inc., 1972.

Waters, Frank, *Colorado*. The Rivers of America. Holt, Rinehart & Winston, Inc., 1959.

The Great Lakes Seaway

Hatcher, Harlan, *The Great Lakes*. Oxford University Press, 1944.

Havighurst, Walter, *The Long Ships Passing*. Macmillan Publishing Co., Inc., 1975.

Hilts, Len, *Guide to Canada*. Rand McNally & Company, 1975.

McKee, Russell, *Great Lakes Country*. Thomas Y. Crowell Company, 1966.

Ratigan, William, *Great Lakes Shipwrecks & Survivals*. Wm. B. Eerdmans Publishing Company, 1960.

The Northeast Coast

Federal Writers' Project, *Maine*. American Guide Series. Courier-Gazette, Inc., 1970.

Gambee, Robert, *Nantucket Island*. Hastings House, 1975.

MacKeen, R. D., *Cruise Cape Breton*. Cape Breton Development Corp., 1975.

Munson, Gorham, *Penobscot*. J. B. Lippincott Company, 1959.

Teller, Walter, *Cape Cod and the Offshore Islands*. Prentice-Hall, Inc., 1970.

The Mid-Atlantic Waterways

de Gast, Robert, *Western Wind Eastern Shore*. The Johns Hopkins University Press, 1975.

Federal Writers' Project:

Georgia. American Guide Series. Tupper & Love, 1954.

South Carolina. American Guide Series. Oxford University Press, 1941.

Virginia. American Guide Series. Oxford University Press, 1941.

Fisher, Allan C., Jr., *America's Inland Waterway*. The National Geographic Society, 1973.

Footner, Hulbert, *Rivers of the Eastern Shore*. Cornell Maritime Press, Inc., reprint of 1944 edition.

Guale, the Golden Coast of Georgia. Friends of the Earth Series. The Seabury Press, 1975.

Stick, David, *The Outer Banks of North Carolina*. The University of North Carolina Press, 1958.

Florida and the Gulf

Federal Writers' Project:

Florida. American Guide Series. Oxford University Press, 1939.

Louisiana. Somerset Publishers, reprint of 1941 edition.

Texas. Scholarly Press, reprint of 1940 edition.

Feibleman, Peter S., and the editors of TIME-LIFE Books, *The Bayous*. Time Inc., 1973.

Gantz, Charlotte Orr, *A Naturalist in Southern Florida*. University of Miami Press, 1971.

The Caribbean Islands

Bayley, Robert, *The Sunny Caribbees*. Duell, Sloan and Pearce, 1966.

Bond, James, *Birds of the West Indies*. Houghton Mifflin Company, 1971.

Craton, Michael, *A History of the Bahamas*. Collins, 1962.

Edson, Wesley, *Terry's Guide to the Caribbean*. Doubleday & Company, Inc., 1970.

Mitchell, Carleton:

Islands to Windward. D. Van Nostrand Company, Inc., 1948.

Isles of the Caribbees. National Geographic Society, 1971.

Morison, Samuel Eliot, *Admiral of the Ocean Sea*. Little, Brown and Company, 1942.

Morison, Samuel Eliot, and Mauricio Obregón, *The Caribbean As Columbus Saw It*. Little, Brown and Company, 1964.

Randall, John E., *Caribbean Reef Fishes*. T. F. H. Publications, Inc., 1968.

Robinson, Bill, *Where the Trade Winds Blow*. Charles Scribner's Sons, 1963.

Ward, Fred, and Ted Spiegel, *Golden Islands of the Caribbean*. Crown Publishers, Inc., 1973.

Woodbury, George, *The Great Days of Piracy in the West Indies*. W. W. Norton & Company, Inc., 1951.

Picture Credits *Credits from left to right are separated by semicolons, from top to bottom by dashes.*

Cover—Luis Villota from Photo Researchers. 6,7—Entheos. 9—Maps by John Sagan. 10—Harald Sund. 12—Jack West. 13—Harald Sund. 14,15—Small insert map by John Sagan, large map by Nicholas Fasciano. 18—Harald Sund—Stephen Green-Armytage. 19—Chris Caswell—map by Nicholas Fasciano; Doug Wilson from Black Star. 20,21—Entheos; Art Hemenway. 22—Entheos. Map by Nicholas Fasciano. 23—Entheos. 24—Map by Nicholas Fasciano; Bruce Calhoun. 25—Pete Smyth—Lyn Hancock; Bruce Calhoun. 26,27—Roy Montgomery; Stephen Green-Armytage—Ronny Jaques from Photo Researchers; Roy Montgomery; Stephen Green-Armytage. 28—Diane Beeston. 31—Terrence Moore. 32,33—Maps by John Sagan. 36,37—William Garnett from TIME-LIFE Picture Agency; Alexander Lowry from Photo Researchers—map by John Sagan; Richard Rowan from Photo Researchers; Stephen Frisch from Photo Researchers. 38,39—Lois J. Kennedy—map by John Sagan; William E. Mackintosh; Chris Caswell. 40,41—Map by John Sagan; David Muench; Jim Amos from Photo Researchers—Chris Caswell. 42—Stephen Green-Armytage for SPORTS ILLUSTRATED. 43—Stephen Green-Armytage for SPORTS ILLUSTRATED. Map by John Sagan. 44—Dick Davis from Photo Researchers—Stephen Green-Armytage for SPORTS ILLUSTRATED. 45,46,47—Stephen Green-Armytage for SPORTS ILLUSTRATED. Map on 45 by John Sagan. 48—David Hiser from Photo Researchers. 50,51—Map by Nicholas Fasciano. 54—Chris Caswell—Robert E. Walters. 55—Jack West—map by Nicholas Fasciano; Carolyn West. 56,57—David Hiser; Margaret Durrance from Black Star—Joern Gerdtts from Photo Researchers; map by Nicholas Fasciano. 58—Tomas Sennett—Fred J. Maroon from Photo Researchers. 59—Fred Leavitt from Van Cleve Photography—Bruce Roberts from Rapho/Photo Researchers; map by Nicholas Fasciano. 60—Michael Philip Manheim. 61—Tom McCarthy—Hank Morgan; map by Nicholas Fasciano. 62—Map by Nicholas Fasciano; Walter Iooss Jr. 63—Virginia Johnston—Angelo Lomeo. 64—Map by Nicholas Fasciano; Walter J. Kenner. 65—Walter J. Kenner. 66—Gerald Brimacombe. 68

—Photo by Robert. 69—Heinz Kluetmeier from TIME-LIFE Picture Agency. 70,71—Maps by John Sagan. 74,75—Gerald Brimacombe; John Crabb—map by John Sagan; Jim Brandenburg; Gerald Brimacombe. 76 through 79—Tomas Sennett. Map on 77 by John Sagan. 80—Daniel Wiener. Map by John Sagan. 81—Daniel Wiener. 82,83—Michael Mauney. Map by John Sagan. 84 through 89—Kryn Taconis. Maps on 84 and 86 by John Sagan. 90—David Rosenfeld from Photo Researchers. 92—Sebastian Milito. 93—Fred Ward from Black Star. 94,95—Small map at left by John Sagan, large map by Nicholas Fasciano. 98,99—Russ Kinne from Photo Researchers—map by Nicholas Fasciano; John Lewis Stage from Photo Researchers; John de Visser—Barbara K. Deans. 100, 101—Neil Kagan—map by Nicholas Fasciano; Russ Kinne from Photo Researchers; Sonja Bullaty. 102,103—John Lewis Stage from Photo Researchers; James B. Murphy—James B. Murphy; Ernest Baxter from Black Star. 104,105—Everett C. Johnson from DeWys—Stephen Green-Armytage; John Lewis Stage from Photo Researchers. 106—Fred J. Maroon from Photo Researchers—Michael Philip Manheim from Photo Researchers. 107—Michael Philip Manheim from Photo Researchers—map by Nicholas Fasciano; Andy Carr from Photo Researchers. 108, 109—Virginia Carleton from Photo Researchers; Peter Miller from Photo Researchers—Arnold Meyers from Photo Researchers; Alfred Eisenstaedt. 110,111—John Achley; Christopher H. L. Owen. 112—Dennis Hallinan from Freelance Photographers Guild—map by Nicholas Fasciano; Stanley Rosenfeld. 113—Lois J. Holeywell. 114—M. E. Warren. 117—Norris D. Hoyt. 118,119—Small map at left by John Sagan, large maps by Nicholas Fasciano. 122—M. Woodbridge Williams—M. E. Warren. 123—Tom Hollyman from Photo Researchers; map by Nicholas Fasciano. 124—M. E. Warren. 125—Robert de Gast. 126,127—Stephen Waterman from Photo Researchers; Frank J. Miller from Photo Researchers—Stephen Green-Armytage; map by Nicholas Fasciano. 128,129—Norris D. Hoyt. Map by Nicholas Fasciano. 130,131—Al Henderson; Fred J. Maroon from Photo Researchers

—Tom Hollyman from Photo Researchers; map by Nicholas Fasciano. 132—Dan Guravich from Photo Researchers—Ron Sherman. 133—Map by Nicholas Fasciano; Frederick C. Baldwin from DeWys. 134—M. E. Warren from Photo Researchers. 136—Red Marston. 137—Dan Guravich. 138,139—Maps by John Sagan. 142—Tom McCarthy. 143—Slim Aarons from Photo Researchers—map by John Sagan; Tom McCarthy. 144,145—Courtesy Florida Department of Commerce; Rick Frehsee—map by John Sagan; Bill Schill. 146—Gary Miller. 147—Stephen Green-Armytage for SPORTS ILLUSTRATED—map by John Sagan; Edward Slater. 148,149—Leo Touchet from The Photo Circle. Map by John Sagan. 150,151—Map by John Sagan; John Lewis Stage from Photo Researchers. 152—Slim Aarons from Photo Researchers. 154—Stanley Rosenfeld. 155—Ernst Haas. 156,157—Maps by John Sagan. 160,161—Bill Robinson; Slim Aarons from Photo Researchers—map by John Sagan; Stanley Rosenthal from DeWys. 162—Bill Robinson. 163—Luis Villota from Photo Researchers—map by John Sagan; Ron and Valerie Taylor. 164,165—John Dominis from TIME-LIFE Picture Agency; map by John Sagan—John Dominis from TIME-LIFE Picture Agency; Fred Ward from Black Star. 166—Fred Ward from Black Star—Virginia Carleton from Photo Researchers. 167—Fred Ward from Black Star—Ernst Haas. 168,169—Dick Davis from Photo Researchers; Ted Spiegel from Black Star. 170,171—George Holton from Photo Researchers—Gerald Brimacombe; Bill Robinson.

Acknowledgments

Portions of this book were written by Peter Wood. The index was prepared by Anita R. Beckerman. The editors also wish to thank the following: Robert Alderice, Galveston, Texas; Ray Cannon, Los Angeles, California; Cpt. W. M. Carroll, Streckfus Steamers, St. Louis, Missouri; Jingle Davis, Coastal Information Officer, Georgia Department of Natural Resources, Brunswick, Georgia; Eldred and Barbara Ellefson, Washington Island, Wisconsin; John Frye, Editor, *Waterway Guide*, Annapolis, Maryland; Dr. Charles E. Herdendorf, Center for Lake Erie Research, Ohio State University, Columbus, Ohio; Halsey Herreshoff, Boston, Massachusetts; Norris D. Hoyt, Newport, Rhode Island; Dave John, Biologist, Louisiana Wildlife and Fisheries, New Orleans, Louisiana; Walter J. Kenner, Naturalist, DeLand, Florida; Dorothy Kirkpatrick, Regional Editor, *Waterway Guide*, Baton Rouge, Louisiana; Ken Lauer, Outer Banks Fishing Safaris, Buxton, North Carolina; Harvey B. Loomis, New York City; Al Mastics, Boating Editor, *The Plain Dealer*, Cleveland, Ohio; Carleton Mitchell, Annapolis, Maryland; Jack Morehead, Superintendent, Isle Royale National Park, Houghton, Michigan; Larry G. Pardue, Horticultural Society of New York, New York City; Jim Roe, Past Commodore, Great Lakes Cruising Club, Chicago, Illinois; John Rousmaniere, Associate Editor, *Yachting*, New York City; Lee Stausland, Englewood, New Jersey; Barney Turner, Little Current, Ontario; Keith Wilson, Chief of the Waterways Division, Department of Natural Resources, Lansing, Michigan.